Illustrated by Susan Carlson
Edited by Tanya Boyd
Translated by Lois Tietzel

2004
Goals Unlimited Press
Huson, Montana

© Eckart Meyners
November 2004

Front cover art and interior illustrations by Susan Carlson.

Library of Congress Cataloging-in-Publication Data
Meyners, Eckart.
  Effective teaching and riding : exploring balance and motion / by Eckart Meyners.
    p. cm.
  Includes bibliographical references and index.
  ISBN 0-9748373-0-X (pbk. : alk. paper)
  1. Horsemanship—Study and teaching. 2. Horsemanship. I. Title.
  SF310.5.M49 2004
  798.2'3'071—dc22
                                          2004020843

PRINTED IN THE UNITED STATES OF AMERICA

Goals Unlimited Press
c/o Equestrian Education Systems
25155 Huson Road
Huson, MT 59846

CONTENTS

Foreword vii

Preface ix

Introduction xiii

Principles of Effective Teaching and Riding 1

Rider 15

The Rider as a Complex Being	15
How Riders Learn—Active Riding	18
The Meaning and Complexity of the Mind	22
Importance of Motion in Learning	24
Role of Observation	26
Motivation	27
Further Influences on the Rider	28
Riding as A Dialogue	31
Perspectives on Motion	32
How Does the Horse Understand the Rider's Signals?	35
The Dialogue Between Horse, Rider, and Instructor	37
Summary on the Dialogue Concept and the Holistic Approach to Teaching and Riding	40
Riding as Learning Motion	41
Coordination and Agility	41
Anticipation of Motion	45
The General Basic Structure of Athletic Motions	46
Cyclical and Non-cyclical Motions	47
Combining Motions	49
Characteristics of Motion	52
Analysis of Motion as Seen From the Outside	55
Analysis of Motion as Seen From the Inside	56
Summary	63

Riding as a Game of Balance	64
Physical Balance	64
Balanced Muscles	67
Psychological and Mental Influences on Riding	75
Having Fun Yet?	75
Concentration and Focus	76
Positive Thinking!	77
Letting Go	79
Fear	79
Aggression/Frustration	86
Seat	94
The Correct Overall Seat	96
The Correct Position of the Head	101
The Correct Position of the Head, the Neck, Shoulders and Arms	104
The Correct Position of the Torso	110
The Correct Position of the Pelvis	116
The Correct Position of the Legs	122
Additional Influences on the Rider's Seat	124
Rider Warm-up	140

Instructor

Fundamentals of Teaching	143
Important Aspects for Lesson Planning	147
Making Decisions	147
Lesson Requirements	151
Horse and Rider Demographics	151
Socio-cultural and Educational Considerations	152
Knowledge of Developmental Stages Regarding, Coordination, Flexibility and Agility	152
Content Analysis of Riding Lessons	158
Didactical Reasoning in Lessons	159
Methods in the Dialogue Concept of Horseback Riding	159
Methods in a Holistic Approach	159

Observation and Mental Training	164
How Observation Helps Us to Feel	165
Supporting Riders' Appreciation for Holistic Connections	166
Instructors Must Teach Students to Feel	166
Methods to Improve the Development of "Feel"	168
Instructors Should Not Overwhelm Their Students with Requirements	168
Opposing Motions are Important in Order to Better Understand Actual Motions	169
Pictures Instead of Commands	170
Focusing a Student's Attention Internally	171
Planning the Course of a Lesson— The Written Lesson Plan	172
Basic Lesson Structure	174
What Instructors Need to Know—Qualifications	176
Sound Technical Skills	176
Teaching Styles in the Arena	177
Communication Skills	177
Play and Flexibility	180
Use of Mistakes	181
Use of Exercises	182
Keep it Simple	184
Lessons for Instructors are Instructional Too!— Evaluating Yourself	185
Criteria to Consider When Evaluating a Riding Lesson	185
Criteria to Consider When Evaluating a Lesson Regarding the Education of the Horse	186
Criteria to Consider When Evaluating a Lesson Regarding the Education of the Rider	187

References 188
List of Exercises 192
Appendix A (Sample Diagram 5) 194
Appendix B (Sample Diagram 6) 202
Index 204
Balance in Motion ® 211

FOREWORD

AFTER DECADES OF RIDING, teaching and attending riding clinics, I have found that it is not often that someone in the horse world comes up with something truly unique and effective. Most of what is out there is simply a rewording or repackaging of old theories and methods, some more helpful than others. It is very rare to discover someone who has come up with something so effective that it dramatically challenges many of our pre-conceived notions and past experiences.

Eckart Meyners is that rare individual who has developed a method for teaching riding that is so remarkably original and effective that there are no words to adequately convey the value offered to riders and horses. "Revolutionary" may sound dramatic, but it may be the most appropriate word, for Eckart's methods make a dramatic difference in the horse almost immediately by focusing on the rider's ability to flow in harmony with the horse's natural motions. Best of all, this immediate improvement comes with very simple, effortless exercises that take a few minutes to learn and execute. Lasting improvement results from continuing practice of these new "feelings."

Eckart's impetus for developing these ideas to help riders become more effective was years of frustration watching riders inadvertently getting in the way and blocking their horses' abilities to move naturally. He was further frustrated by traditional teaching methods that focused on commands instead of locating and fixing "blockages" in the riders. Like other athletes, riders need to return to their own, natural motions.

It has been said many times that Eckart can do in minutes what takes other instructors years to accomplish, if they ever do. This is not an exaggeration. Fortunately for all of us who ride and love horses, Eckart's methods work and work quickly. They seem almost "magical," but in fact are an integration of ancient philosophies with modern research in the fields of learning and motion, now applied to horseback riding.

I want to thank Eckart for allowing us to support and introduce his philosophy and research to American equestrians, imparting the principals I have seen create happy partnerships between horse and rider. Effective Teaching and Riding is an introduction to his practical and well-founded principles.

I would like to thank Jürgen Billich for his dedication to a clear translation of this material, and am grateful to the respected educators who have joined me to brainstorm, discuss and create programs and products utilizing Eckart Meyners' principles for instructors and riders; Beth Beukema, Dana Butler, Lendon Gray, Eric Horgan, Lazelle Knocke and Jocheen Schleese.

And I would like to thank you, the reader, for caring enough about your horse, your riding and your students to read this book. It will absolutely change the way you look at and think about riding and riding instruction, and the fine art of harmony of motion to be found on the back of a horse.

JILL K. HASSLER-SCOOP
author of *Beyond the Mirrors, In Search of Your Image, Equestrian Education,*
and *The Riding Experience & Beyond*

PREFACE

TEACHING HORSEBACK RIDING and learning how to ride are complicated processes that need to be made more understandable for both instructors and riders. The high level of complexity in horseback riding is due to the constant interaction between horse, rider and instructor. The goal of this book is to explore these interactions with the intent of developing more effective instructors, riders, judges, and examiners.

Instructors in this country have been largely left to their own devices to discover what "works" as far as helping riders to improve. Judges and examiners as well have not always had countrywide standards with which to evaluate either riding or instruction. Some of the concepts and principles introduced in this book will feel very foreign to readers and will require an open mind in order to understand the role they have in developing effective instructors and riders.

The first section, the *Principles of Effective Teaching and Riding*, gives instructors and riders an overview of many of the subjects that we will discuss in more detail throughout the rest of the book. Teaching, riding, judging, and examining require knowledge and integration of principles of education, principles of riding, and psychology. A circular model for riding instruction is presented that graphically illustrates the interactions between the principles and concepts necessary for effective teaching and riding.

Effective instructors give their students specific exercises to improve their riding skills. A rider's actions are transferred to the horse, which means a rider must be able to be decisive yet smooth in his motions so that the horse will react correctly. Both creatures must learn how to communicate through body language. Before this communication between instructor, rider, and horse can occur, the instructor must analyze each rider's different motions and actions, as an individual and also in regard to the horse's motions. A rider's internal learning processes coupled with the rider's ability for motion based on his or her individual body structure and general fitness determine both what and how the instructor will communicate with the student.

All of the above still does not guarantee effective teaching and riding. Instructors must also take into account the role of the rider's mind as well as the horse's brain processes. This is fundamental for teaching a student to ride effectively. Instructors need to consider a person's and a horse's age and have reasonable expectations for both horse and rider based on a comprehensive assessment of the individuals as well as the relationship between them. Furthermore, the instructor must choose the teaching method best suited for the specific pair of horse and rider. Instructors need to discover what motivates their students and find a suitable communication pattern that works for them in order to have committed students and avoid problems during the learning process.

The second section, the Rider Section, explores the rider as a complex being. Riders reading this section will learn about the processes going on in their bodies and minds as they learn to ride. They will also learn how to actively participate in lessons, which will enhance their learning ability. Teaching the rider and the horse to make the right decisions at the right time in every situation, even when the instructor is not present, is the overall purpose of riding lessons.

The dialogue approach to teaching and learning is introduced in this section. Using the "dialogue approach" instructors and riders can discover how rider and horse should communicate with each other to find a balanced relationship and to develop harmony while working together. This approach teaches them to recognize the intricacies of both horse and human and how to interpret misunderstandings that may occur during the communication process.

Motion, coordination, agility, and balance are also explored in depth in this section regarding their role in riding and teaching. The uniqueness of these concepts for horseback riding stems from the necessary interaction of the motion, coordination, agility, and balance of the horse combined with the motion, coordination, agility, and balance of the rider.

Riding movements and motions are not only physical processes, but are largely rooted in the mind and other inner processes. The importance of good flow between the right and left sides of the brain and the development of the rider's sense of "feel" are discussed. This chapter also offers suggestions for riders on how to improve their horsemanship by being more in sync with the horse and channeling their energies efficiently. Fear and aggression can sometimes result from miscommunications or other life circumstances. Both instructor and rider should be conscious of the effect that fear and aggression have on learning and also be aware of the circumstances that cause these problems. Horseback riding should be a positive experience for instructor, rider, and horse.

Lastly, the Rider Section details riders' motion patterns and possible difficulties that may arise with them, beginning by defining the rider's seat and what makes it effective. In this chapter background information on how problems develop will be explained for the instructors, and riders can learn how to make their body language more understandable for the horse.

The Instructor Section is mainly intended for instructors because it deals with the organization and planning of lessons. It also describes the necessary qualifications of effective instructors and the developmental stages that humans go through regarding physical abilities. Of course, riders are also welcome to read this section because it will help them understand how complex an instructor's work truly is. Riding instructors must be experts regarding both horses and humans.

Instructors need to be able to use various methods while giving lessons. They should always try to meet the individual needs rider and horse, because not every rider (or horse) learns in the same manner. Various methods for instruction will be presented in this book that are based on the understanding of horseback riding as a dialogue between horse and rider. Through observation and mental training—which improves awareness—student riders can help instructors in their efforts to make lessons a harmonious and effective dialogue between all participants.

INTRODUCTION

PEOPLE OFTEN THINK OF THEORY AND PRACTICE as being completely unrelated in many fields. There are the theoreticians who spend their time studying and developing theories about something and then there are the practitioners who are actually out in the field doing the work. This dichotomy seems to exist in almost every subject, and horseback-riding instruction is no exception. Throughout history many theoretical books have been written on the subject of horseback riding, and as well, many people have simply gone out and mounted a horse and figured out how to "ride" without ever picking up one of the theoretical manuals.

> **Effective Teaching and Riding** *is based on the premise that practice should be influenced by theory but should go beyond simple transmission of theory to the rider. In order for instruction to be truly effective, principles of* **learning** *must be integrated with the principles of* **riding**.

This book is based on the premise that practice should be influenced by theory. In order to be effective teachers and riders, we need to incorporate some theory into our practice. Theory cannot stand alone, but neither can practice stand alone. Sometimes the theory that we need comes from outside the equestrian arena, such as incorporating effective instructional theory into teaching horseback riding lessons. This integration of various theories with practical experience will result in an overall "applied theory" of effective teaching and riding. The intention of this book is to introduce readers to this concept of applied theory through offering practical suggestions for riding and teaching that are firmly grounded in educational and equestrian theory.

AN OBSTACLE

As a long-time teacher of sports education theory (also known as physical education theory), I became used to the skeptical looks my audience gave me as I started to lecture at a conference. They were being forced to sit through what they considered to be useless information on becoming a riding instructor. They were of the opinion that the only way to learn how to ride was to actually do it, so what was this academic man from the university going to tell them about giving lessons? I often heard complaints like, "Education theory hangs over the practical side of riding like a big, dark cloud." Lesson planning seemed to be a foreign phrase in the riding community, and people appeared to believe that it was an uncommon, irrelevant basis for practical lessons. "We all know the horseback riding traditions and that's enough!" other participants groaned.

As I listened to all of their protests I thought about how I could convince them that it is necessary to think about and incorporate these theories of education into the practice of giving riding lessons. Education theory is important for them, I thought, because it would eventually help them to be more effective instructors for their students.

A FIRST ATTEMPT

My attempt to convince them of the importance of education theory began with Diagram 1. Principles of riding exist, which include the Stages of Education for the Horse. These principles of educating a horse are an application of the best physical education theories in the world with regard to the motions of a horse. The problem is that these principles do not give the riders any help in learning, so the principles of riding alone cannot lead to effective learning for the rider. General riding theory does not address, let alone recognize, the individuality of both rider and horse; it is not practical. If theory and practice do not complement each other problems arise. Each rider and each horse have distinctive individual strengths and weaknesses that must be recognized in order for effective learning to occur. The development of principles of riding education, which would enable the instructor and student to communicate effectively about the principles of riding, would be more likely to lead to effective teaching and riding.

The traditional principles of riding help the horse, but not the rider. Riders' vast abilities and their individual weaknesses and limits are scarcely considered. Horseback riding books thoroughly describe how to lead a horse through exercises, but the intricacies of the highly complex human being are not included in these books.

This typical scenario (Diagram 1) begins with planning to teach a riding lesson. It then moves to consideration of the principles of riding, such as the Stages of Education for the Horse recognized by the German National Federation. These principles are largely based on the ideal progression of the horse and rider. With these principles in mind, the instructor approaches the rider, but not as an individual. The rider is seen as a generic being that is to fit into the overall plan. With these components in place, the methodical steps for the lesson are finally decided.

The riding lessons described by traditional riding theory are based on a perfect rider and a perfect horse.

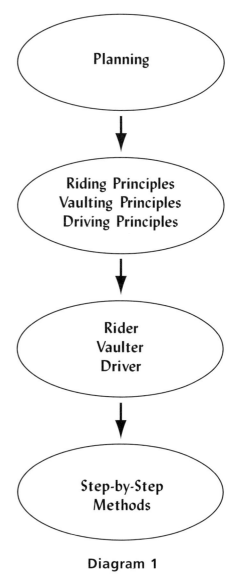

Diagram 1

The projection of a given scenario onto a real horse and rider cannot work because there is no such thing as a perfect rider or a perfect horse. Rarely will a horse and its rider perform exactly as described in one of these traditional lessons. There is no room in the theory for individuality. Many of these lessons do not work because they put the horse in the forefront and put the human in the background. The horse may show progress, but we do not see any improvement in the rider's motions and action. We have to ask ourselves, "What exactly do instructors know about human beings? What do they know, for example, about their wide range of different motions and daily bad posture habits?"

A SECOND ATTEMPT

Historically horseback riding made the horse the first priority in lessons and education—which, under the circumstances, was the right thing to do. In earlier times people's lives were often more centered on horses, so they learned horsemanship from the time they could walk. The motions came naturally to them and it was not necessary for them to learn how to dialogue with the horse; they relied on their instincts and sense of feel to know how to interact with the horse. Over the centuries horseback riding has developed into a competitive sport and a hobby. A large percentage of riders today did not grow up with horses. They did not have the opportunity to learn about horsemanship at a very early age and also often did not have a large variety of motion experiences as children. As a result they are very inexperienced in motion and feeling when they begin to ride. Thus, in order to have an effective riding lesson, instructors must recognize and pay attention to the differences between the past and the present, especially in regard to young riders. We must consider human beings as highly complex and intricate creatures. As instructors, our lessons must be based on individuality to such an extent that the rider is able to follow the logical steps in the session and "unlock" the horse's and their own potential. The lesson must be taught in such a way that the rider can be just as effective when she or he returns home and rides without the instructor.

The following statements refer to Diagram 2. When planning a riding lesson using this method, the instructor begins with a foundation of structured, systematized principles of learning which consider each student as an individual. The student is considered first, and then the instructor moves on to incorporate his or her knowledge of the principles of riding *as they apply to this particular student* into the lesson. This first combination of principles helps the instructor to understand the inner processes going on in both horse and rider. From this point the instructor can choose specialized exercises to aid in the development of the rider.

The second oval in this diagram, representing overall principles of learning, simply enhances instruction, allowing traditional horseback riding principles to remain a vital part of lessons.

I will share a little story to illustrate the importance of educational principles in teaching riding. In training seminars I often begin by asking the question, "When can a child actually benefit from horseback riding instruction?" (Psychology defines "childhood" as the phase from birth until puberty, approximately 11 or 12 years). The answers always cover a broad range of ages and are accompanied by many different explanations. Each person bases his response on his own experience. Each person's experience differs, however, because each instructor has taught children with different skill levels and various backgrounds. Therefore it is not possible to generalize based on people's individual responses, derived from practical experiences.

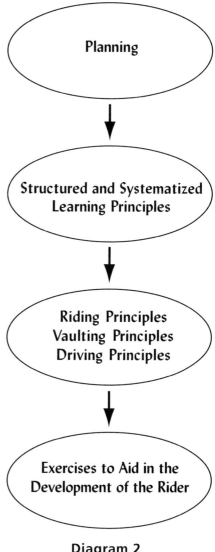

Diagram 2

Theory, based on years of research, helps teachers be more confident when making decisions about answering this question. In order for horseback riding instruction to be effective, a variety of aids must be used and combined. The rider must be able to use the legs, body weight and hands individually as well as coordinating them without interfering with the motion of the horse. Developmental psychology has found in the study of children that the control of arms, hands, legs and feet stabilizes by the age of approximately 10 years so that erratic, sudden and bulky motions all but cease.

We have gained important knowledge for riding lessons from these studies. Since a child younger than 9 or 10 years cannot control their leg muscles or the reins as accurately as necessary for safety and comfort during horseback riding lessons, these formal instructional sessions should not be started too early. After the age of 9 or 10, once the fundamental developmental abilities are in place, systematic lessons can begin. Beforehand, however, a child should gain general physical experience from play and playful exercises, which allow the child to develop the ability to understand basic motor skills. A good foundation in basic motor skills is vital for the later development of a child's physical abilities. Riding is just one of the many activities that require these fundamentals. If a child is experienced in basic motor skills, he or she can learn a more complex motion, like riding a horse, much more easily and much faster than a child without a good foundation in the basic motor skills.

As a child begins to learn to ride, he also must learn how to balance himself on the horse in various situations and tempos, how to use his pelvis and how to counterbalance the weight of the body with his arms and legs. At the same time, a child must be able to mimic the horse's rhythm in order to stay well seated. These skills have to do with two kinds of balance, upright balance and balance while moving (*see Rider Section, page 65*), as well as the development of rhythm and being one with the animal and its motions. Sitting in a saddle is not like sitting in a chair. The balance needed for riding a horse is very different than the balance needed for sitting in a chair. When on the horse, the child must stay seated, but in a dynamic way. This foundation in balancing skills should be developed through playing games and doing other playful exercises, just as the basic motor skills and coordination of motions were developed. It is very important that this stage in a child's development not be cut short (from Miesner/Meyners 1997, Neumann-Cosel-Nebe 1990).

HOW THIS BOOK CAN HELP INSTRUCTORS, RIDERS, JUDGES, AND EXAMINERS

After reading the practical example illustrated above, you might have realized how developmental psychology can expand the understanding of the principles of basic horseback riding and help instructors effectively plan and carry out their lessons. Without integration of the educational principles, instructors might try to teach a 7-year-old child in the same manner that she would teach a 15-year-old adolescent. Both instructor and student might experience frustration as a result. The next question is, "Why should training seminars include the Principles of Effective Teaching and Riding? What is so complicated about learning to ride that makes these principles so necessary?" This book will attempt to answer these questions and explain how these principles specifically pertain to a rider's education.

I would like to thank Jill Hassler-Scoop for her dedication to bringing my instruction methods to American equestrians. Since discovering our common belief that riding is about the 'whole' person, Jill has dedicated her time, money and energy to making my principles available outside of Germany. This book is due in large part to Jill's enthusiastic support. We hope you enjoy the results.

ECKART MEYNERS

PRINCIPLES OF EFFECTIVE TEACHING & RIDING

Introduction of Principles

In the following section I would like to introduce the aspects that make up the Principles of Effective Teaching and Riding and explore why teaching riding is so complicated that it needs specific principles on how to do it. Although this text only encompasses horseback riding, the principles are also applicable to carriage driving and vaulting. The circular shape of Diagram 3 illustrates the interconnectedness of each of these principles. The rider (or driver or vaulter) stands in the middle of the circle and is influenced by each of the various principles. This means that the rider's practical outcome or skill level in riding the horse is affected, for better or for worse, by each principle. The principles themselves also interact with and influence each other. By standing in the center, the rider takes responsibility for his or her own learning process; riders must be aware of the various principles and the role they are playing in their own personal situation. The arrows are double-ended to show that just as the principles have an effect on the rider, the rider can also affect the principles. The instructor is listed twice among the principles around the circle, once on the top left and once on the top right. You will notice that the arrows connecting the instructor and the student are darker and thicker than the other arrows; this is because the reciprocal relationship between instructor and student is key to effective teaching and riding. The instructor has two roles to play; one is that of mediator of motion and one is that of educator. The other principles are divided up based on these categories and are listed on their respective sides. It is most important, however, to understand that it is impossible to isolate any one principle from the others; they are all interrelated and interconnected. Thus is the complexity of humanity and the challenge of the riding instructor!!

THEORY FOR GIVING INSTRUCTION

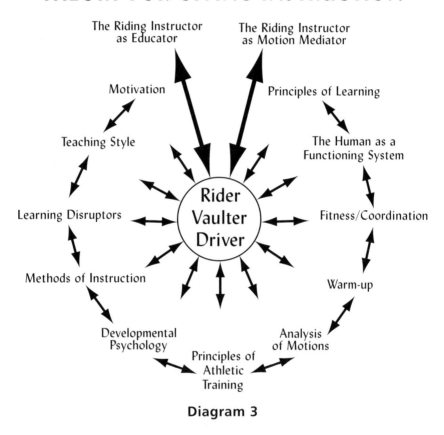

Diagram 3

THE INSTRUCTOR AS MEDIATOR OF MOTION
Instructors must have experienced what goes on inside of a person when sitting on the horse in order to transfer this knowledge of motion to the rider. This knowledge cannot be written down; it is known in the body.

Horseback riding is more complicated than any other sport simply because the instructor has to deal with two moving, breathing, living creatures who are both very unique. This individuality must be acknowledged and accepted in order to make the riding experience an enjoyable and progressive one. Riding educators must, therefore, be *mediators of motion* for both rider and horse. The instructor, having experienced what it feels like to be on a horse and performing a certain motion, must be able to transfer this knowledge of motion to the rider. This is often done through teaching basic position, which places the rider in a situation to feel a new motion in a correct way. Then the rider has to integrate this new feeling into all of the other motions taking place in her body. The rider initially learns to follow the horse's motions, but as the rider develops in ability and skills, she learns how to use her body to influence the horse's body and motion. Horse and rider should not be separated since one's weakness can be compensated by the other's strength throughout the learning process.

The main goal of riding lessons should be to establish a symbiotic relationship between horse and rider. This requires well-founded knowledge (expertise) in the principles of horseback riding as well as very sensitive riding skills so that the instructor will be able to "ride with" the student. This "inner-riding" during a lesson enables the instructor to "feel" the student's smallest mistake or divergence from the correct motion before it becomes apparent to the eye. This "inner-riding" or "riding with" the student is essential to helping the student develop the correct feel in her body for whatever task is being learned. By understanding motion (*see Motion in Rider Section, page 32*), evaluating riders' own motions and abilities, and using exercises on and off the horse to help the rider develop a feeling for motion (*see Rider Section*), instructors fulfill the role of being mediators of motion.

Riding and the "Inner Eye"

The idea of "riding with" the student has to do with the "inner eye." During this process the instructor can "feel" every little nuance of the rider's motion. (This specific concept is also known as the "Carpenter-Effect" or, today, as *visualization*—from Ennenbach 1989). Once specific riding motions are deeply anchored in a rider's psychological system (brain, emotions and muscles) they do not disappear, even during long periods of not riding. This has also been called "muscle memory." While the brain is involved in initially learning the motion, once the rider's muscles and feeling system takes over, the brain does not have to think about the motion anymore. The body simply can perform it. It is on this level that a skilled rider observing another rider making the same motions that have been ingrained into his own mind and body can literally experience the motion with the person who is actually performing it, even from his armchair.

> *This has also been called "muscle memory." While the brain is involved in initially learning the motion, once the rider's muscles and feeling system takes over, the brain does not have to think about the motion anymore. The body simply can perform it.*

This type of learning goes hand in hand with mental training and good observation. Motions are not actually performed, but they are thought through as if they were actually being performed. Training this way makes it much easier for a person to improve because his motions become subconscious and he does not have to first think it all out before he performs an action; he can simply perform it because it is ingrained in him.

> *Instructors who use this visualization technique, which allows them to "ride with" their students, can anticipate mistakes and intervene before they occur. This offers the student a better chance of developing the correct muscle memory and "feel" from the beginning.*

Back to Instructors

Instructors must have incredibly sensitive riding skills in order to be able to correct students *before* their mistakes are evident. They must use the visualization technique, which allows them to "ride with" their students. Instructors with these special skills can anticipate mistakes and intervene before they occur, thus allowing the student a better chance of developing the correct muscle memory and "feel" from the beginning. During a lesson where a rider is learning a new motion, the instructor can initially talk the rider through the correct body position and aids needed in order to obtain a certain feel, and then the instructor can remain silent while the student experiences that feel and it becomes a part of her muscle memory.

This method is different from many typical riding lessons where the instructor "rides through" the student the entire time. While the horse and rider may appear to achieve great things through following the instructor's commands, the rider will not develop the appropriate muscle memory or "feel" without some quiet time to experience the feel and allow it to transfer to muscle memory. Students who have instructors who give commands all the time, as if the students were puppets on strings, will not be able to achieve the same level of performance on their own once their instructor goes home. Students whose instructors help them to a place where they can feel a particular motion and then allow the student time to integrate that feeling into their muscle memories will find that they are able to ride at the same level between lessons as they achieve during lessons.

> *A rider needs some quiet time to "feel" the motion; this allows the rider to develop the appropriate muscle memory.*

> *In addition to being accomplished physical educators, instructors must also be good teachers in general, meaning that they should be able to communicate with riders calmly, easily and firmly. Every rider has special communication and motivational requirements. Therefore, instructors must be very skilled in these areas.*

PRINCIPLES OF LEARNING

Riding lessons must be based on good educational methods and lead students to become independent, showing them how to make good, quick decisions in every situation. Therefore, instructors should not just bark out commands like a drill sergeant, but should include the students in the learning process. Instructors and students have to work with each other; they must be a *team*. The students must be able to ask questions, make suggestions, introduce their own ideas, etc., and these must be discussed together and then worked out. *This is called "active learning" and is described in further detail in the Rider Section.*

THE HUMAN AS A FUNCTIONING SYSTEM

Even with an extensive background of theoretical knowledge about physical education, including motion, feel, coordination, etc., instructors also need to consider that each person is a different kind of learner, possesses a different body structure and has a lifetime of different muscle memories stored in their body. If equestrian physical education is to function properly, it cannot simply rely on the theoretical basics, or on a universal pattern of teaching and learning that is intended for every rider. It must be adapted to the individual.

> *Each rider is a different kind of learner, possesses a different body structure and has a lifetime of different muscle memories stored in their body.*

Theory about proper position for riders is usually based on an assumed ideal body shape and balanced muscles. Most riders do not have a perfectly balanced muscle system or an ideal body shape. Therefore, instructors must become familiar with how each rider actually functions; which position of the pelvis in the saddle is best, which muscles might tighten up, which muscles need to be stretched, which brain reflexes need to be retrained, etc. It is not enough to simply teach the theoretical ideal position to all students. All theory is useless without the practical knowledge of how to apply it for each individual student. In light of this, instructors must perceive their students not only as learners, but also as complex body systems (a muscle-bone-tendon-ligament system). The instructor must figure out how to apply the theory to each rider's unique body type. *The Rider Section will discuss in more detail the most common problems seen among riders.*

THE ROLE OF FITNESS AND COORDINATION

Each person not only has a different body type, but also different abilities when it comes to fitness and coordination. Fitness is made up of strength, quickness ("speed"), and endurance. Each rider must possess at least minimal abilities in all three areas in order to sit correctly and to control the horse.

How often do instructors have problems getting a desired response from their students? The instructors make an enormous effort with their well-intended advice, but their students are too exhausted to respond. Their bodies simply cannot exert the necessary strength any longer. In these situations students are not able to react quickly to the horse's actions because the nerve endings in the muscles are not responsive enough.

While strength, quickness, and adequate endurance are necessary, they are not the only requirements. Riders also need coordination and agility. A good foundation in coordination and agility is even more important than good fitness for having a good "feel" for the horse. By "coordination" I mean the synchronized, homogeneous and parallel motions of all body parts. The rider must be well schooled in coordinated actions in order to have a successful dialogue with the horse. Good coordination allows proper differentiation between balance, rhythm, visual and spatial orientation, and feeling (with the muscles). These are all essential foundations for learning horseback riding.

Furthermore, riders must be agile and flexible enough to adapt to the horse's movements. Special exercises off of the horse can help improve flexibility, balance and agility. The more flexible and balanced a rider is, the better she will be able to move with the horse and the more control she will have over her own body and that of her horse. (See Meyners 1996, 2003/1, Miesner / Meyners 1997.) *The Instructor Section explains how children learn coordination in different developmental phases.*

PREPARATION FOR LEARNING, PRACTICING AND TRAINING PROCESSES — Warm-up

Every rider warms her horse up before she begins to ride him in a lesson. However, *riders* seldom do a warm-up themselves or physically prepare for a lesson at all, even though preparation is one of the most important elements of sport activity. For a complete guide to an efficient warm-up before lessons (either alone or with an instructor) see Eckart Meyners' *Exercise Program for Riders: Simple and Effective,* 1st ed., 2003.

ANALYSIS OF THE RIDERS' MOTIONS

In order for instructors to be effective in fixing mistakes or deviations that riders make, they must first discover the true root cause of the problem. If an instructor simply looks at the movement that the rider is making (or is lacking) and attempts to fix the problem at that place in the rider's body, it is very likely that a change will not occur. Most problems have their root somewhere else in the body or mind than where the problem becomes visible. Instructors must be able to analyze the motions of the rider, inside and out, using morphological criteria, in order to determine where to begin to make a change. Morphology is the study of "form" – for riders it refers to the study of the rider's position and the interaction between position, motion, and effective interaction with the horse. Throughout the rest of this book we will refer to the rider's motions rather than to a rider's movement because it is at the level of motions, which are interconnected and integrated throughout the whole body, that change can take place. The Rider Section discusses various rider deviations or mistakes and their corrections based on a holistic approach to understanding rider motion.

PRINCIPLES OF ATHLETIC TRAINING

As mentioned above, a good foundation in coordination and agility is more important than good fitness for having a good "feel" for the horse. Nevertheless, riders should strive to be fit and healthy by cross-training (jogging or cycling, for example) at least twice a week for a minimum of 30 minutes. Their pulse should climb and remain at about 140 beats per minute.

Another option for cross-training is going to a gym and working with their personnel, who are specialized in finding muscle deficits and building them up. Equestrians are athletes, as are their horses, and it is important to include an appropriate level of athletic training for each individual horse and rider. This is seen most intensely in the sport of eventing, where horses and riders must be extremely fit in order to safely meet the demands their sport puts on them. In all equestrian disciplines the level of athletic training necessary will increase with an increase in skill within that discipline, so a horse and rider competing internationally at Grand Prix level dressage will need a much different athletic training program than a horse and rider schooling first level dressage for fun at home.

Speed is another part of the principles of athletic training. The term "speed" with regard to riding means that the rider should be able to respond immediately to any of the horse's unpredictable actions, such as spooking or running off. This is called *reaction speed*. Riders' knees and thighs (their leg aids) should react immediately so that they can remain mounted. They should also be able to effectively coordinate leg and rein aids.

THE INSTRUCTOR AS EDUCATOR

A riding instructor has the responsibility to pursue the field of education in addition to studying the equestrian field. The field of education includes principles for preparing and presenting materials with a method that is clear, concise and thorough. An educator understands how people learn, various presentation methods, individual learning needs and practical psychology. Thus an effective riding instructor is a well-informed educator as well as an accomplished equestrian. All of the principles on the left side of Diagram 3 are related to the cognitive/psychological aspects of learning and instruction. It is necessary for riders and instructors to involve these capabilities in riding education, but it is also necessary for information gained through these paths to be transferred across the diagram to the right side so that they can be put into motion on the horse.

MOTIVATION

If a rider is not motivated, she will not want to find a solution to problems that occur during a lesson. There are many influences, both positive and negative, on a rider's motivation. The rider's intentions and the situational conditions are the two most important aspects of motivation.

If a riding instructor is not able to make the learning environment or situation emotionally stimulating, the actual learning will not go very well. Instructors must also carefully consider the abilities of both rider and horse in order to have a successful lesson. The quality of the horse plays a role in the level of a student's motivation. If the student thinks, from the very beginning, that he cannot manage the horse, then he will not be able to learn well. Horses, too, can have similar feelings toward their riders. They may simply refuse to work with certain people. Therefore, instructors should pay close attention to how their riders and horses get along.

Students have different motivations for learning to ride. Working with students and riders who have a desire to move, learn the functions of riding, experience a little adventure and become accomplished equestrians is much more satisfying than working with students without these goals. Motivated riders have a strong inner drive, which makes them capable of taking constructive criticism. However, if students are there to simply "look good" it will be very difficult to communicate with them. They may tend to project their own problems and deficits onto the horse and instructor. This situation creates an unproductive learning environment. Also, other characteristics, such as dealing with success or failure, influence a learning environment. *You will find additional information on motivation in the Rider Section.*

TEACHING STYLES IN THE ARENA
As we all know, teaching styles have a considerable influence on how we learn. The different styles of teaching horseback riding can either hinder or encourage learning. Usually riders prefer a rather easy-going style to a commanding, very controlling style. Constant commands tend to create stress for the rider, thus obstructing effective learning. Naturally, there are also those students who have grown accustomed to their instructor's gruff tone and seem to work fine with this style of instruction. These different interpretations of an instructor's tone and style point to the fact that each student is different and should be taught appropriately. In other words, instructors need to get to know their students and try to create a personalized learning environment. *You will find more information on teaching styles in the Instructor Section.*

DISRUPTIONS TO THE LEARNING PROCESS
Many psychological and mental issues in the rider such as being over focused, worrying, and feeling stressed out can disrupt the learning process. One of the most common disruptions to the learn-

ing process that instructors must deal with is fear. Fear is not only present in horseback riding, but also in other aspects of life. At times I wonder why some people want to learn to ride when they obviously are very afraid. Fear of horses and learning to ride just do not go together. Fear makes the muscles tense up, which in turn delays reactions and dulls the senses. It is similar to a horse that is internally tense. As long as the horse balks, there is no chance of riding him. The same goes for humans; if fear has you in its grip, you cannot get anywhere.

Many things can cause fear. There can be issues with spatial orientation problems, problem-solving difficulties, physical ailments, fear of failure or blame, etc. Today there have been enough studies done on the subject of fear that instructors should be familiar with the possible sources. They can then use this information to discover what might be causing their students trouble and how they can help them deal with it. In this case, instructors would not be teaching riding but instead would be taking care of their students' psychological conditions, something that requires a large amount of patience and sensitivity. The rider has to first overcome his fear and regain his positive outlook before he can begin to learn horseback riding. *The Rider Section addresses fear and other disruptors to the learning process in greater detail.*

METHODS

In horseback riding there are two main categories of methods of instruction: 1) the *command*-oriented method, and 2) the *experience*-oriented method. According to my understanding of teaching and learning horseback riding, the rider must play an active role in the learning (and teaching) process, which is only possible through the experience-oriented method. Several researchers have come to this same conclusion. Two of their theories are discussed elsewhere in this book: 1) active learning, and 2) learning as a dialogue between horse and rider, (*see more information in Rider Section pages 18 and 31*).

The Command-Oriented Method

As you might assume, we will not discuss the command-oriented method in detail since it does not have much relevance to our way of teaching riding. Nevertheless, situations can arise in which commands are needed, for example with pure beginners and with riders who are just guessing about how to handle their horses and who may be in a dangerous situation. The following are a few beneficial uses for the command-oriented method. This method works best when combined with a majority of experience-oriented instruction, so that the commands are kept short and to a specific task or focus, and never take over the entire lesson.

- Defining a goal, under the guidance of an instructor, and improving riding abilities
- Developing horses' and riders' required physical abilities and coordination
- Developing a rider's ability to imagine an action (verbally; with the necessary assistance)
- Practicing steps in an exercise or practicing the entire exercise (such as leg-yielding)
- Improving parts of exercises or entire exercises using correction
- Reinforcing a lesson by combining new material with already learned material

The Experience-Oriented Method

Experience-oriented learning (called the experience-oriented method) places the emphasis on what the rider is experiencing rather than on what the instructor is commanding. When used correctly and consistently it results in the rider's developing a feel for the *horse's motions* and *learning to work independently with the horse*. These two skills are necessary in order for the rider and horse to be able to make correct decisions in every situation, regardless of the presence of the instructor.

Riders are not supposed to simply copy any given riding seat. The rider will not be pressed into a mold of the "ideal" riding position. Instead, a rider should be able to develop specific and individual goals for himself and his horse by working closely with his instructor. Each step must be planned around the rider's individual feel for the horse. This type of lesson does not incorporate strict commands, but utilizes teamwork instead. The rider is an active participant in the learning process from the very beginning. Here are the components of the experience-oriented method:

- Communication between instructor and student.
  - Discussing the good parts and the parts that need improvement in any motion of horse or rider.
  - Open dialogue about any frustrations the rider or instructor may be feeling.
- Creating a lesson based on a horse's ability and a rider's skill level with increasing difficulty based on development of correct muscle memory.
- Constructing individual solutions according to a rider's own ideas and feelings.
- Helping a rider to become aware of his "inner image" (feeling a motion) – the instructor is an objective moderator who helps a student by asking questions about how he felt and how he solved the problem.
- Utilizing and expanding previously learned lessons by combining them with new ones (reinforcement).
- Integrating ideas and feedback from a wide range of sources, based on the results.

DEVELOPMENTAL PSYCHOLOGY

Instructors find themselves having to take on a multitude of different roles over the course of a day, and thus need to be well skilled across many situations. For example, one moment instructors may be trying to teach a technical skill and a moment later they need to handle a physical or emotional crisis. Instructors frequently teach across the whole age and developmental spectrum, from young children to older adults. As well as having an understanding of the physical development of riders, successful instructors must also be knowledgeable in developmental psychology. It is important to have examined the intricate developmental phases that occur during childhood and adolescence. If instructors are not educated in this area, they will more than likely have trouble interpreting verbal and body language correctly. Understanding the psychological development of their students will help instructors be better teachers as well as mentors, role models and coaches, who are able to inspire, energize and sustain their students' interest in and motivation for their sport.

CONCLUSION

All the subjects that we have discussed cannot and should not be separated from each other. Teaching horseback riding is a very complicated phenomenon and can only be successful when it is firmly anchored in riding knowledge, experience, theory and skill. So, before I forget, here is one of my favorite sayings: "There is nothing more practical than a good theory." Instructors should not shy away from challenges in their lessons, but rather *deal* with them!

In the following chapters I will not deal with every subject area that has been mentioned. I have chosen a few topics that I think are crucial for the practical aspect of teaching. This book is meant to be a foundation and a starting point for further study. The interested reader can explore each topic introduced here further. The most important concept to understand is that effective teaching and riding is complex and requires knowledge and integration of many topics beyond just the principles of riding.

RIDER

The Rider as a Complex Being

The rider is a complex being. Learning to ride involves all aspects of the person; it is not enough to simply try to mold the rider into the perfect form as you would a lump of clay, and it is not sufficient to simply tell the rider everything that she needs to know, as you would input information into a computer. Riders are complex, with variations in motivation, goals, communication abilities and styles, body types, ages, history of mental and physical "injuries," fitness abilities, flexibility, coordination, intelligence, connectedness, learning ability and styles, and sense of feel. On top of the rider's complex individuality is the horse's complex individuality and on top of this is the uniqueness of each rider/horse pair. Trying to create only one way to teach and learn horseback riding is simply impossible. Our goal with this section is to explore the many ways that riders are unique, complex beings, and how their individuality affects common challenges that arise during lessons or practice rides. Knowledge of this information is a pre-requisite for giving effective lessons.

Individuality

It is not enough to simply understand the theory of the "correct" seat. Riders and instructors must also understand and accept the uniqueness of each horse and rider combination. Each person is a different kind of learner and possesses a different body type, muscle system, etc. If equestrian education is to be effective it cannot rely on a fixed set of commands or positions. As a result of a rider's unique body, each rider will have various imbalances in either structure or muscle development that will be important to their ability to learn to ride. Instructors must become familiar with how a rider actually functions and not assume that all riders are the same. A particular rider's pelvis will function best in a certain position in the saddle, which may not look exactly the same as other riders' positions. Riders' internal and external muscles will tighten up depending on their structure, strength, balance, and previous experiences and muscle memories. If an instructor relies solely on theoretical knowledge without practical, individualized knowledge, he or she will never be effective. Instructors must perceive their students as learners and also as complex body systems (a muscle-bone-tendon-ligament system). Only from this understanding can rider deviations be detected and corrected, leading to effective motions, and thus to effective riding.

Each person has not only a different body type, but also different abilities and aptitudes regarding strength, quickness and fitness. A minimum amount of each of these is necessary in order to sit "correctly" and to learn to control the horse. Beyond this minimum requirement riders' abilities vary greatly and instructors need to take these levels into consideration when developing lesson plans and setting goals with their students. If students become physically exhausted they will not be able to respond to the instructor's suggestions because their bodies cannot exert the desired strength any longer. In these situations students are not able to react quickly to the horse's actions because the nerve endings in the muscles are not responsive enough. Instructors can help their students to find appropriate cross-training exercises that will allow them to develop the fitness needed to feel and handle the horse well during the training sessions.

As well as appropriate strength, quickness, and fitness, riders also need coordination and agility. By "coordination" I mean the orderly and simultaneous motions of all body parts to meet a certain goal. The rider must be well-educated in coordinated motions in order to have a successful dialogue with the horse. Riders must also be agile and flexible in order to adapt to the horse's movements.

Each individual will arrive at their lessons with more or less of these abilities, depending on many factors going back to childhood. Instructors must be aware of any deficits in these areas and work with their students to develop these areas if a student is lacking. This can alleviate a lot of a student's frustration because it may be that the student can understand what the instructor is asking, but cannot make their body coordinate the necessary aids or flex into the needed position. When an instructor recognizes this and works to help a rider through these problems, progress will be made.

How Riders Learn—Active Learning

In the section on the Principles of Effective Teaching and Riding, the idea of active learning was introduced. Active learning is opposite to command-oriented learning where the instructor gives commands and the rider reacts to that external influence. In active learning the instructor creates a task for the rider, who then has to plan internally which motions to use to complete the task. The following section explains the inner-processes going on inside students during active learning in greater detail. Human actions are goal-oriented, motivated, planned and controlled; they are conscious actions that originate from within the person. This is where we will begin in examining the rider's inner-processes more closely.

A rider's action is:
- Goal-oriented: Riders work on perfecting certain actions they wish to master.
- Motivated: Riders want to improve on the knowledge and skills they already possess.
- Planned: Riders create a picture in their head of how to perform an action.
- Controlled: Riders strive to make as few mistakes as possible and to make the correct decision in every situation. However, students cannot correct themselves while performing an action; they must depend on the instructor (who has a perspective from outside of the action) to help them correct their mistakes or deviations.

Conscious actions: All inner-processes in the rider are filtered through the brain's center for feeling/sensing. Instructors strive to teach students to work from the inside, not from the outside. If students work from the inside out, they can learn to recognize and correct their mistakes and deviations on their own.

> *Instructors must strive to teach students to work from the inside, not from the outside.*

The sequence of human actions can be divided into three phases:
- Orientation phase (including an initiation phase)
- Execution or performance phase
- Outcome phase

This describes the overall sequential order of human actions; however, these phases do not always occur immediately one after the other. During the performance phase constant feedback from the outside produces the need for a new orientation. The complexity of understanding and performing an action make learning a difficult process. Therefore, we will break these phases down into parts and use an example:

The following example will illustrate the basic inner learning process. This basic principle of learning will help explain every other learning situation in riding.

We have a beginning rider who can trot well, has started to canter using the lunge line, and knows the following aids:

- Half-halt
- Shifting his weight to the individual seat bones
- Use of the outside guarding leg slightly behind the girth
- Use of the inside driving leg at the girth
- Supple, following seat
- Loosening of the inside rein during the canter transition

After the horse has been warmed up, the instructor gives the student the task of getting the horse to canter, off the lunge line. With such an open-ended exercise the student is forced to think and decide when, where and with which aids he should ask his horse to canter. The student is not being commanded, but instead is actively participating in the learning process.

ORIENTATION PHASE

In order to find the solution to this exercise the student must consider the various areas of the riding arena to decide where to ask the horse to canter:

- Long sides
- Short sides
- Corners
- Somewhere else in the ring

The Rider's Inner Processes

The rider may be thinking something like this: "In the corners I have a better chance of getting the horse to canter because he will automatically turn and I can use the bit more easily. This makes it easier for him to begin to canter."

Choice of Aids

Once the rider decides on a place in the arena to ask for the canter, the rider must decide which aids to use, based on previous experience gained on the longe line. The rider may decide, "I will use my outside guarding leg and my inside driving leg. By pulling my outside leg back, my weight will automatically shift to the inner seat bone. The other aids are also helpful, but I will use them later. I can't use all the motions at once. If these aids work, I will apply the others afterwards."

Interpretation of the Situation

The long side, the short side and the corners impose outside controls on both horse and rider. By showing the horse the rail or the wall of the arena, the student will try to make it easy for the horse to transition from trot to canter. Furthermore, by using the seat weight aid (the inner seat bone) the horse is brought off balance and can only regain balance again by moving into a canter. It is important to choose the most comfortable aids for the horse so that it can "understand" what the rider wants it to do (mentally and physically).

Students' actions should be goal-oriented in that the student should understand what he is trying to accomplish. A student who wants to please his instructor and his horse by choosing the right aids to complete the task will be motivated to plan accordingly. Goal-orientation and motivation are evident in this situation because it is clear that the student has not yet mastered the exercise, but has, nevertheless, understood what he must do to solve the situation.

An easy lesson not requiring any problem solving does not really motivate students. However, a new lesson should not be too advanced for the student, either. The student must be able to apply her knowledge, but, at the same time, not be overwhelmed. In this case, the student has a chance at figuring out the task. During this stage of learning a new skill the student must be closely observed by the instructor, but not told exactly what to do. The only way to consistently improve a student's skill is to systematically and methodically build upon previous knowledge in each lesson. Only then can a rider learn to be independent.

During the orientation phase students should imagine the exact sequence of events; they should play the situation out inside their head asking, "Which aids should I use?" This is where the left brain is allowed to be active, in helping to plan an action. After the rider has decided on the best location in the ring and the aids he wants to apply, the left brain needs to allow the right brain to execute this planned sequence of events.

EXECUTION PHASE

Because riders not only have to deal with their own motions, but also those of the horse, it is not uncommon that the first attempt fails. In our example, the rider might make a mistake, which would cause the horse to also make a mistake. It is the instructor's job to understand the complexity of the situation and act accordingly.

Beginning or novice riders cannot always perform every action correctly, nor immediately recognize or feel their mistakes. They cannot immediately feel any deviations in the sequence of carefully planned events simply because their perception for such things is not yet schooled well enough. That is why the instructor is there; to help the rider learn how to *feel* these deviations and correct them.

Nevertheless, instructors should not immediately correct students during the execution phase, but rather ask them if they felt any discrepancy or inconsistency in their actions. The student's answer will let the instructor know whether or not the student felt the motion correctly and if the student's image of the sequence of events was sufficient. If the student's performance and his analysis do not coincide, instructors can assume that either his knowledge of theory is inadequate or his ability to "feel" is not clear enough.

OUTCOME PHASE
The outcome phase is the most important phase because it is the phase for refining actions. Feedback is vital for this process to function correctly.

Our beginner, as described above, cannot yet "feel" the correct motion or his deviations because they are not yet anchored in his muscles (or imprinted in his brain). Because of this he can only partially "see" himself from the "inside" (by *feeling* with his muscles) and by the same token partially see from the "outside" (with his *eyes*). In general, since riders only see a very small percentage of their own motions, their visual observation of themselves is not adequate. In order to have a view of the whole picture, riders must be able to *feel* these little deviations and mistakes from *within*. Being able to *feel* is precisely our goal.

Riders are not able to realize their mistakes right away in the beginning stages of learning new actions. For this reason and because riders are usually unaware of the circumstances causing their mistakes or deviations, the instructor's objective viewpoint and corrective advice (constructive criticism) are very important.

The Meaning and Complexity of the Mind
In the human brain there is a part of the brain that plans motions and there is a part of the brain that "does" the motions, or puts them into action. The planning part of the brain, commonly referred to as the "left brain," is the thinking, logical part of the brain and is housed in the newer cerebral cortex of our brain. Learning does begin to take place here, but effective learning does not stop here. The "doing" part of the brain, the "right brain," is the sensing and feeling part of the brain and involves structures that are much older and and more reflexive than the cerebral cortex. In order for a motion to

take place properly, the "left brain" must plan it, and then step back and allow the "right brain" to conduct the motion. Another way of thinking about it is that the head is the commander of motion and the feeling is the executioner of motion (see Gallwey 1990). These two parts of the brain are connected and must work together for learning and motion to occur. To understand this connection it is important to look at the different parts of the brain in a simplistic way. The following chart shows the relationship between what Gallwey calls the head and the feeling.

LEFT BRAIN—*Head/Cognition*	RIGHT BRAIN—*Feeling*
Nearsighted	Farsighted
Analytical	Holistic
Gets involved in everything	Just lets things happen
Rational	Emotional
Objective	Subjective
Very concentrated	Relaxed
Methodical (one thing after the other)	Comprehensive (everything at once)
Scientific	Artistic
Logical	Illogical
Introverted	Extroverted

When riders perform at their very best observers can be heard commenting, "She makes it look so easy – as if it's second nature!" or "He's riding without even thinking!" These comments have one thing in common; they are describing a state of performance in which riders are not being controlled by the planning/logical part of the brain. Instead, they ride intuitively, feeling and sensing the horse and their own body. Of course, they are fully conscious of their actions, but they do not have to think about them. If riders "let themselves go" while riding, they can *feel* the horse, see jumps and the distances between them, and simply perform as they have done thousands of times under supervision. These riders know how to cue their horse and which muscles to use without thinking about it. As the motions unfold, they do not think about what they are doing or let the logical reflex take control. They do not let their "flow" become interrupted or their thoughts get in the way by constantly double-checking or judging their motions. *They just ride.* They forget the rest of the world and dissolve into the horse and become one with its rhythm.

This "dream-like" state of *feeling* the motion and not thinking about it is the entire purpose and goal of having a *dialogue* with the horse. In order for riders to communicate through motion and with another creature using their senses they must first learn to feel and sense their own motion. People must recall this kind of sensing that they knew as a child; everyone experienced it when they learned to walk and talk as children.

Constant interaction between riding, assessing feeling, analyzing, making new goals and discussing actions with the instructor helps students' performances become more exact. Their actions become engrained and imprinted in their brains through feeling. Students are able to increasingly catch their own mistakes and describe them, find the causes, and eventually, with the guidance of their instructor, correct them. The brain simply gives the cue and it "happens."

This type of interaction allows instructors not only to get an overview of their students' abilities to explain, to question, to correct, to describe and to perform; but also an overview of their abilities to absorb, understand and store information.

These learning processes have more to do with the subconscious than with the rational conscious. Subconscious impulses originate from the spinal cord and brain stem. Conscious impulses originate from the cerebral cortex. People (and those who want to become good horseback riders) must learn to let go and let things happen instead of constantly thinking about them. The development of an educated sense of feel is what makes this possible.

Importance of Motion in Learning

We must move in order to learn! This principle has been long understood and put into practice by multitudes of equestrians, but in recent years people have turned more and more to trying to learn without as much motion. Some people do not have the benefit of riding lessons but have access to a horse, and so learn to ride simply by riding. When they make the wrong decisions they either fall off or the horse does not do what they want it to do, and when they make the right choices and movements, they move with the horse in the direction they intended to go. With the benefit of instruction this process of learning through doing can be even more effective, as the instructor can guide the student's process of trial and error to keep them on the right path.

It makes sense to think about motion as being necessary for learning to ride, since riding IS motion. Motion awakens many parts of our brain that are necessary for learning anything, not just how to ride. This is why it is much easier to learn and memorize your dressage test or jumping course if you actually ride the pattern, or perhaps walk through the pattern on your own feet, or even draw the pattern on a piece of paper. When you just read about something or look at a movement, without associating an inner motion with it, very limited numbers and types of nerve cells are activated in your brain. There is no way for your body then to connect what you have thought about or looked at with an inner motion that you may want to perform. The only way that you can move any part of your body is if a message is sent through your central nervous system via the network of nerve cells that you have developed through past motion. So by performing a motion you are helping to form and reinforce those neural pathways that make possible all of the various motions you may want access to at some point.

When you are learning a new motion, this is why it takes several attempts to perform it correctly. Your nerve cells have not set up the appropriate connections needed for that motion, so the message is sent first through old pathways, which may not be the most efficient or correct. However, through interactions with the environment (in the case of riders this includes involvement of the horse and instructor) the student will finally be able to perform the new motion. If she brings her attention to what it feels like at that moment to be moving in that particular way, she will solidify in the muscle memory those neural pathways, and the next time she wants to perform that motion, her brain will be able to send the messages to the body parts via the newly laid down, efficient pathways to create the same feeling.

For example, if a rider is learning the sitting trot, her first attempts at sitting and following the motions of the horse's back will probably result in tension and uncomfortable bouncing. Up until this point the body's learned response to bouncy motion of any sort is probably to tense up against it and try to get away from it. There are no nerve pathways from the brain to the body to tell it to relax when the sensory nerve cells are blaring "Bouncy motion! Bouncy motion!" However, through the help of her instructor, perhaps some longe lessons, and some exercises to teach her body new possibilities for motion, the rider will finally find one or two strides where the trot is not so bouncy. She will probably notice this herself, as it will be much more comfortable, but her instructor may also help by telling her when she has it "right." If at this point she can bring her awareness to her body and just remember that feeling of comfort, that sensation will be picked up by the sensory nerve cells and carried to the brain. Instead of shouting, "Bouncy!" they will instead report, "Comfortable and smooth!" and the motor nerve cells will no longer carry the message to "tense up" out to the muscles. Instead, the other motor nerve cells that just happened to be sending the messages to relax at that moment will be reinforced, and the next time the student rides the sitting trot, she will be more likely to find a few more strides that are comfortable.

This learning could not happen simply through thinking about it, or explaining it to the student. No matter how many times an instructor told the student how to sit in the sitting trot in order to be able to follow the horse's movement instead of bouncing against it, she will not get it until her nerve cell pathways have a chance to experience it and develop the appropriate connections in the brain.

Role of Observation

Based on what we discussed above, there would seem to be no role for observation in learning to ride, but this is not at all true. Observation can be a very important part of the learning process, but it has to be done properly. There is a difference between just watching something, and watching it as if you were doing it where you actually feel similar sensations that you would feel if you were performing the action. Observation by itself, just watching another person perform a motion, will not be of much benefit unless you allow those visual cues to convert to sensory cues. This activates the nerve connections that will be needed when you actually do perform the motions.

Going back to our sitting trot example, if a student were to watch hundreds of people riding the sitting trot, she would not become any better at it herself *unless* she watched them riding while imagining herself sitting in the saddle and "feeling" what each of those riders might be feeling at that moment. This type of observation or visualization actually does activate the exact same nerve connections as would be used when the student is riding the sitting trot herself. This is why visualization can be so powerful, for better or for worse! If you think about riding your cross-country course, but picture yourself falling off at a certain jump and imagine the pain of hitting the ground you will be much more likely to actually have that experience when you ride it, or at least to have a refusal or run-out because your body is anticipating what you visualized. However, if you visualize your cross-country round perfectly, feeling the way your horse's body rises over each jump and how perfectly your galloping stride meets each fence, you will be much more likely to actually ride the course that way because your muscles have actually had real practice at doing it right!

Motivation

Why do people ride? Working with students and riders who have a desire to experiment with motion, to learn the principles of riding, to experience a little adventure, and to become accomplished equestrians is much more satisfying than working with students who do not have these goals. Motivated riders have a strong inner drive which makes them capable of hearing and learning from constructive feedback. On the other hand, if students are there to simply "look good" or because they have been pressured into taking riding lessons it will be very difficult to communicate with them to make any difference in their riding ability. They may tend to project their own problems and deficits onto the horse and/or instructor instead of taking responsibility for them. This situation creates an unproductive learning environment.

There are many motivators for people who ride. Some people simply enjoy being around horses, some people enjoy the challenge of learning something new, some people find it relaxing, and some people like the thrill of competition. It does not matter WHAT the motivator is, but both rider and instructor must be aware of the motivator and agree to structure their lessons and practice around that motivator. A rider who rides for fun may not want intense lessons aimed at moving up through the levels of dressage, or may not want the jumps to be higher each week. However, a rider who has a solid goal of competing at a certain level will want a goal-oriented instructional and practice program where each day brings them closer to their performance goal. Instructors can help their students become aware of their motivation, and riders also need to educate their instructors about the kind of instruction that works for them and their own personal goals and motivation.

Further Influences on the Rider

Riders live in differing environments that will affect their ability to learn and to ride. Becoming aware of these from the perspective of a rider or an instructor will help in the overall conception of a rider as a complex being.

Nutrition (Eating Habits)

The way people nourish their bodies (their eating habits) has an enormous effect on their energy. All over the world people tend to think that sugar gives their bodies energy. This is true for raw sugar (unrefined). However, refined sugar has the opposite effect. Refined sugar actually robs the body of energy. Unfortunately, most people's nutrition does not supply them with the right energy needed to be healthy and balanced. Mass-production of refined foods with countless additives threatens nutrition and health. Looking at the different kinds of bread, for example, we find that they are full of unnecessary and unhealthy additives. White bread is made with extremely refined flour and white (refined) sugar. "Whole wheat" bread is made with added sugar and conservatives. Today we cannot even enjoy natural foods such as fruit, vegetables, wheat or barley, eggs, seeds, nuts, white or red meats because they have been so tampered with (not to mention the effects of pesticides). Instead of preaching about nutrition, I would simply like to make riders aware of their nutrition and eating habits – especially before and after riding. Nutrition can also have a positive effect on learning!

Water
Water is essential to overall health and to people's ability to learn. Water is what allows nerve cells to function properly, carrying messages from the brain to other body parts and vice versa. It is also the main transport mechanism for carrying other nutrients around the body. A person's total body weight is made up of 45% to 75% water, with leaner people having a higher water content than fatter people. Muscle carries more water than fat, which repels water. Research has estimated the brain's water content at up to 90%. As a rough guideline each person should consume 1 quart of water per 100 pounds of body weight each day, and more when under stress of any kind.

Environmental Influences
Most people have experienced what effect music can have on emotions. Music can produce feelings of fear and it can also make people cry or make people want to jump for joy. Music can help bring people to a higher level of performance and ability. Classical (instrumental) music has a wonderful and powerful effect on people, and it does not have to be loud to be effective. Many horses also seem to enjoy music, especially classical. For some people having classical music playing while they are riding allows them to feel their horse's movements more clearly.

People, themselves, can either have an energetic or anti-energetic effect on others. Consider how you might feel while being yelled at or unfairly criticized. The human aspect of a person's environment can definitely contribute to the energy that person feels and to how well that person can concentrate on the task at hand. If a rider has a critical parent sitting outside the arena watching their lesson, it is likely that the rider may not perform as well or may become frustrated with the horse sooner than they might without this negative influence. On the other hand, having a supportive cheering section when riding at a competition can elevate performance and the rider's personal feelings of satisfaction.

Natural materials or man-made materials can also have an effect on our energy fields. Wooden objects versus plastic objects, precious stone versus plastic jewelry, natural versus synthetic fibers, sunlight versus artificial light, natural ingredients versus artificial (chemical) ingredients in makeup, can all have an effect on our health and learning processes. Even watch batteries attack the bio-chemical processes in our cells and lead to long-term negative side effects.

Riders should become aware of their environment and do whatever they can to ensure that it is healthy and beneficial, so that it acts in a positive way towards their learning ability. For the purposes of this book it is enough to mention these additional environmental factors as influencing the learning process; riders may want to explore any of these areas further in order to develop a fuller understanding of how their own environment might be contributing to their learning successes or roadblocks.

Riding as a Dialogue

Each horse and each rider has a unique "style." No horse moves in exactly the same way, just as no rider moves in exactly the same way. Each person (and each horse) is an individual with a distinctive body, mind and spirit. Instructors, judges and everyone else should observe their motions with this in mind. Riders' and horses' motions are unique. They are *not* homogeneous. The teamwork of horse and rider is key for good riding because it requires them to constantly communicate with each other (the dialogue perspective). This is what leads us to comment on the incredible partnerships that have made history; it is not usually just the horse or just the rider that sticks in our minds, but the combination of the two creating an incredible, harmonious, and often breath-taking performance. Initially people learning to ride might think that the "dialogue" is just one way; they give commands to the horse, like pushing the accelerator or brake pedals in a car, or turning the steering wheel. Those who have not been around animals, and horses in particular, may not appreciate or be tuned in to the information that the horse gives back or the questions that the horse asks of the rider. As human beings we are conditioned to think of a dialogue as involving words, but dialogues can happen (even between two humans) in silence as well. Over time instructors help their students to feel the horse's responses to their aids, as well as to learn to "listen" for the horse's questions and statements along the way. This is the part of riding that keeps most people coming back day after day. Every day is different because two beings each have something to contribute to the overall picture.

> *In order to understand riding as a dialogue between horse and rider we must realize that each partner plays a pre-determined role in a performance situation. Thus, horseback riding is essentially this: the rider creates and conveys signals to the horse through his actions, and, subsequently, understands the reactions of the horse to these signals.*

Perspectives on Motion

There are two main perspectives on motion, the one-dimensional and the holistic. While it is important to understand both, the principles in this book support the holistic perspective.

THE ONE-DIMENSIONAL PERSPECTIVE OF HORSE AND RIDER MOTIONS

Today, teaching horseback riding seems to focus largely on the outward forms of rider and horse. Instructors and judges are almost totally focused on the moment-to-moment changes going on with rider and horse. They only analyze the HOW and WHAT of these alterations: which body part changes in which way and how closely does it match the ideal.

This purely one-dimensional perspective of horseback riding is common across all disciplines and at all levels. It does not, however, respect the individuality of the horse and rider and their choreographed motion together, nor does it analyze their actions adequately. One example of this is in competitions where certain breeds of horse are considered appropriate or inappropriate for the chosen discipline. A horse of an unusual breed may be doing an excellent rendition of the movement, but the superficial form of this horse may not match the ideal form as pictured using the standard breed.

This kind of superficial perspective uses tunnel vision. Just as most beginning riders only understand riding as a purely physical activity, the argument that horseback riding is merely mechanical does not explore the abstract side of riding (*feeling* the horse). In reality the mechanical/physical is always inextricably linked with the abstract/feeling/mental.

Posture, for example, is always connected to a person's whole being, including their inner psychological state and their physical structure and fitness. Each action a rider makes expresses a part of that rider's inner character. This is why an official "correct" seat for all riders (based on external observation only) presents a huge problem. Trying to force every rider into the same mold will not yield the same results of motion and harmony. *(See more on posture on page 125.)*

Teaching methods based on "external analysis" can be described as follows: the rider's motions are controlled by commands from the outside, so that the rider takes scarcely any initiative himself, but rather lets the instructor direct his body motions and position. The problems with this are two-fold. One, the rider will not be able to find this "correct" position again on his own when the instructor is no longer directing him exactly how to do it; and two, placing the horse and rider in the "correct" mold does not ensure that the correct mechanics and feel are happening under the surface. The rider's position, as well as the desired position of the horse's body, has a purpose; to ensure that horse and rider move together in balance and harmony in a manner that builds correct muscles and results in longevity and soundness. The truly correct form for each horse/rider pair will occur when what is happening inside is correct and then results show on the outside. When riders and horses are squeezed into predetermined "correct" molds, the inner workings of their bodies and minds may not be truly correct, and the long-term results will not be the same.

It is therefore fundamental that the *holistic* perspective be applied to horseback riding. Instructors and riders can recognize physiological and psychological problems in the rider by reading a horse's actions. Although this type of research has already been done with humans, it has not yet been done with horses.

THE HOLISTIC PERSPECTIVE OF RIDER AND HORSE MOTIONS

The holistic perspective is based on the principle that riders are not moved by someone or something, but move themselves. Riding, when understood as a self-imposed action, means that a rider acts independently in every situation—expressing his own artistry. In other words, the rider tries to make his own motions (riding aids) correspond with those of his horse in all kinds of situations (indoor and outdoor arenas, forests, over jumps, around barrels, etc.).

> *The holistic viewpoint is based on the principle that riders are not moved by someone or something, but move themselves.*

The holistic perspective requires instructors to understand how riders' and horses' *senses* function in a variety of different riding situations, as opposed to focusing only on their bodies. Instructors must find out *why* a rider employs certain aids at certain times and *when* these times are. The one-sided physiological perspective only analyzes the specific changes in the rider's actions without considering the rider as an individual or the uniqueness of each riding situation. This perspective would not understand that a horse and rider may perform differently under different conditions, whereas the holistic perspective assumes this to be the case. The goal may be to bring these performances closer together, but the holistic perspective begins by assuming differences will be there, asking what they are and why, and then working to resolve any difficulties.

Riders' and horses' motions are processes involving muscles, nerves and minds—important for all intentional actions. The holistic perspective supports the development of these processes in allowing the rider to act intentionally and independently. Under the one-dimensional method the rider never has a chance to act on his own because the instructor controls the horse *for* him!

> *Riders' and horses' motions are processes involving muscles, nerves and minds—important for all intentional actions. The holistic perspective supports the development of these processes in allowing the rider to act intentionally and independently. Under the one-dimensional method the rider never has a chanceto act on his own because the instructor controls the horse* **for** *him!*

How Does the Horse Understand the Rider's Signals?
Riding is simply a matter of conversing with the horse; a symbolic "conversation," not the actual act of verbal conversing. A rider asks the horse a question by using his aids; the horse answers with his behaviors and shows his rider how he understood the question (the rider's action). If the horse did not understand the question (the action or cue), the rider must repeat it. The horse may also "ask questions" by initiating behaviors the rider did not ask for, such as speeding up, leaning on the reins, or turning his head to the outside. In these situations the rider must answer by using her aids to correct the horse. More questions are communicated as actions or motions until the rider and horse communicate effortlessly with each other. The rider must also listen to the horse to find out what he can already do (what he can offer) and what he needs to work on. This "conversation" can, however, turn into unpleasant confusion if there are too many misunderstandings or disruptions. Over time a horse and rider can come to understand each other's "questions" better and better so that the actual aids given become smaller and smaller. This is where the true beauty of equestrian sport appears; the outside observer cannot see the conversation between horse and rider and yet they are in perfect harmony performing all kinds of movements, highly coordinated and balanced.

REASONS FOR MISUNDERSTANDINGS BETWEEN RIDER AND HORSE
When riders are very inexperienced, horses can easily misunderstand them. If a rider is not in good physical shape (weak muscles, poor coordination or poor conditioning), he will use the wrong body language (aids) and transmit false signals to the horse. Also, a new horse/rider pair will require time to come to understand each other's methods of communicating. In addition, riders may not possess enough "feeling" to react sensitively to the horse. This lack of feeling can be caused by too many command-oriented lessons, which hinder the rider from using her senses (feel) to understand and control her horse. Verbal communication alone cannot come close to accommodating all the motions in horseback riding. This principle sets parameters on the

amount and type of an instructor's verbal communication (see Instructor Section, page 177).

It is absolutely imperative that the communication systems of both horse and rider are on the same level to achieve a true dialogue. If this is not the case, one of them must be far enough ahead to be able to lead the other so that the "language barriers" can be surpassed and misunderstandings avoided as much as possible. Thus a beginner rider should ride a very experienced and solid horse who knows the correct aids and responses, and a young horse should only be ridden by an experienced rider who likewise knows the correct aids and is skilled at explaining to the horse what she wants. The dialogue between horse and rider (the rider's aids and the horse's actions) is very complicated and must be understood as an interactive motion. The instructor's role is to facilitate communication between rider and horse in every situation, realizing that miscommunications are learning opportunities for horse and rider, yet can also become frustrating loops without proper facilitation and coaching.

Horseback riding is simply the exchanging of information between horse and rider through signals, or aids. The meaning of these signals is created through the ongoing dialogue between horse and rider. Each signal has its assigned meaning (to motivate a new behavior, to correct a non-desired behavior, or simply to support an ongoing desired behavior); however, they can be used slightly differently by each rider and be understood differently by each horse.

> *Horseback riding is simply the exchanging of information between horse and rider through signals, or aids. The meaning of these signals is created through the ongoing dialogue between horse and rider. Each signal has its assigned meaning (to motivate a new behavior, to correct a non-desired behavior, or simply to support an ongoing desired behavior); however, they can be used slightly differently by each rider and be understood differently by each horse.*

The Dialogue Between Horse, Rider, and Instructor

There is another important dialogue in the riding arena besides the dialogue between horse and rider, and this is the ongoing dialogue between horse, rider, and instructor. The quality of communication, both verbal and non-verbal, in this dialogue will determine the overall long-term success. An instructor facilitates open and honest communication by involving the student in the learning process, discussing what he is seeing in the rider and the horse and what steps he thinks are necessary to move towards the agreed upon goals. The rider's role is to communicate what she is feeling and thinking both about the horse and about the instructor's comments. If the rider is feeling frustrated and is able to verbalize this to the instructor and if the instructor is able to hear her and respond empathetically and thoughtfully, that frustration can become an important part of the learning. If, however, the dialogue is not strong between instructor and rider, that frustration will become an inhibitor to learning. Additionally the horse will sense the instructor's intentions, mood, and authority, and will react to it. School horses come to know instructors very well, and a true dialogue can exist between them that can be helpful to a beginner student. More will be said about the dialogue between rider, horse, and instructor in the Instructor Section of this book.

RIDING MEANS BEING SELF-INITIATED

As we have seen, learning riding is all about learning motion. Learning motion is learning to understand the interaction between rider and horse as a dialogue. To understand this process, riders must be able to act independently. As independent people riders produce certain motions (aids) and transfer them to the horse. If riders experiment with different motions to discover what is correct for that horse, they can build a muscle memory library full of "perfect" (or correct) performances. This will then help in each future situation where that particular motion is desired, as the rider has a large amount of stored past experiences to draw on. This is different for the rider who is not self-initiated, or who is dependent on the instructor to tell them what to do all the time. These riders, when faced with a similar situation in the future, will not have any muscle memories stored to refer back to, and may feel at a loss for what to do.

For the most part, riders must be able to estimate their own abilities. They must learn how to feel whether their abilities are equivalent to the challenges of any given riding situation. Instructors should take the role of coach, letting their riders know if the decision to use a particular motion was correct or not. The more sensitive riders are, the more they will be able to recognize when they or their horse made a mistake. They will also be able to understand more about why the mistake occurred. Being self-initiated does not mean being left alone to one's own devices. It means being supported by the instructor on the journey of discovery, but owning the journey as one's own. Instructors advise and help their students through difficulties and problems with suggestions and feedback, through the dialogue process. Helping a student to become self-initiated is a unique didactic concept that will truly make a difference.

WHAT HAPPENS INSIDE THE RIDER?

Learning to ride is a process. As spectators we only see the external products of internal processes. Riders are constantly becoming more aware of their motions on (and with) the horse. They are always improving their ability to calculate their own actions and the resulting actions of the horse. They are constantly learning, through dialogue, if their actions and those of the horse are the correct actions for the situation at hand, and they are learning any necessary corrections.

"In order to work well with the horse a rider needs to be balanced and comfortable. Then the dialogue can begin to happen through the aids and motion initiated by the rider. This is possible through subtle movements and slight changes in the center of gravity and in the points of contact with the horse. However, attempting to apply external forces will ultimately result in failure. The application of external force is commonly practiced in lessons (for example, with the commands 'shoulders forward' or 'shoulders back'), without a visible improvement in the rider's bodily behavior. How often do riders fall back into their old posture again?" (Meyners 1996, p. 113). Riders need to develop more self-esteem and to own the changes they make. When the rider understands the reasons for the changes, then the rider works with the instructor and the horse to find a solution. This solution will last much longer than any changes made as a result of external forces from the instructor.

LEARNING TO RIDE WITHOUT REGULAR INSTRUCTION

Of course, it is possible for a person to learn about motion processes through practical experience without the constant instruction of a riding coach. This may take more time and requires a quiet, safe area in which to work with the horse. This kind of learning works best for riders who have already achieved a certain level of competence and confidence, and have the maturity to handle this more advanced learning environment. Putting beginner riders on horses without instruction can be dangerous and is unlikely to yield many positive results as far as developing the motions necessary to come into harmony with the horse.

This type of independent learning requires a great deal of time. A rider must be aware of this so that he can have an idea how to plan the session most effectively with his instructor. A rider in this situation must also have a plan as to *how* he will go about accomplishing his goals. He must use *self-talk* effectively in order to be able to converse well with the horse. If a rider can judge his own behavior well (by being sensitive, feeling and practicing inner-observation), it is possible (and desirable!) for him to become more and more independent of his instructor over a period of years. This should be the goal of every instructor as well; to create independent, confident, competent riders!

> *The goal of every instructor should be to create independent, confident, competent riders!*

On the other hand, it can also be argued that since horseback riding is so complex (having to deal with not one creature but TWO), complete independence from an instructor can never be accomplished. While horse and rider are at different levels of achievement, it may be possible for one to learn from the other (i.e. as in an experienced rider bringing a young horse up to his level of riding, or an inexperienced rider learning from an experienced horse), but once they are both on the same level, it may take an instructor to help them to continue to make progress together.

Summary on the Dialogue Concept and the Holistic Approach to Teaching and Riding

It is always amazing to me to observe how mechanically most students seem to ride, without allowing themselves to be in tune with what they are feeling and sensing. So often I observe *lack of sensitivity* in students—proving time and again how infrequently riders actually listen to themselves and their horses. For example, when they make a transition from a walk to a trot, the horse begins with his outer leg like he is supposed to, but the students have trouble identifying this motion and may not be able to pick up the correct posting diagonal. It seems to me that many riders do not *sense* what is going on underneath them. The holistic perspective of horseback riding and being self-initiated deals with precisely this quality of sensing. Sensing the horse and finding the right answer in every situation is crucial in riding.

I hope I have not frightened any readers away with my description of these intense learning methods. Riding is a truly fun sport and can be even more satisfying when learned in this way. If instructors try to teach their students from a purely physiological standpoint, their lessons will not be as fulfilling as they should (and could) be. Command-oriented lessons only confine a rider's motions to rigid standards, press them into pre-determined molds and make achieving goals more difficult.

Riding as Learning Motion

Being able to see and judge motion is a difficult task in sports that are centered on motions, such as dressage, ice-skating, gymnastics, etc. In these sports motion is observed as a sequence of individual frames (still pictures of a fluid motion). This often leads to differences of opinion in evaluating riders' performances, since each person sees a different sequence of frames. At riding competitions each judge and each person in the audience has different criteria in mind when watching a performance. They all have differences of opinion. Sports that are focused on end results, such as track and field events, or horse racing, do not have this problem. Their accomplishments are precisely measured in centimeters, grams, seconds and milliseconds—there can be no difference of opinion.

The different categories used to study motion are based on the actions of rider and horse. After initially defining and exploring concepts of motion itself, the following sections will define each category of motion and apply them to either the horse or the rider using examples.

Coordination and Agility

An important part of learning motion is developing coordination and agility skills. Some people develop these naturally through appropriate childhood experiences, but others may not have had that benefit and will need to "catch up" in these areas before being able to achieve their full potential as riders.

COORDINATION

Coordination is defined as harmonious functioning of muscles or groups of muscles in the execution of motions. In order for coordination to occur, the right and left sides of our brains must communicate efficiently and effectively. Seen from a biological standpoint, coordination is essentially the parallel performance of controlled muscle actions. Flexors and extensors interact based on reactions in the nervous system. Coordination is referred to as "neuro-muscular" since the brain sends messages to the muscles via the neurons. There are three categories of motor skills that make up coordination:

- Basic motor skills
- Control skills
- Adaptation and adjustment skills

These three basic categories diverge into five specific coordination skills:

- Balancing skills
- Rhythm skills
- Spatial orientation skills
- Kinesthetic judgment skills (sensation)
- Reaction skills

Categories of Motor Skills

Basic motor skills are simply highly coordinated motions. Basic motor skills are learned and remembered in the muscle system, a process called procedural memory. The end result of this process is muscle memory. Once a basic motor skill is committed to muscle memory, the rider does not have to consciously think about each part of performing that skill. In any situation, the rider will be able to perform that skill without conscious effort. Basic motor skills include being able to understand given information, to consider that information and to commit it to memory. The following are all very important for basic motor skills: functions of the eyes, ears, skin and inner ear (the main balance organ), motion sensor abilities (kinesthetic analysis), judging and categorizing abilities, and memory.

Most important in riding are *control skills*, which involve spatial orientation, making decisions based on sensation (kinesthetics), and balancing ability.

Adaptation and adjustment skills refer to one's ability to find creative and flexible solutions to new situations involving motion. They also involve balancing skills, reaction skills, spatial orientation, and sensation (kinesthetics).

Specific Coordination Skills

Balancing skills are defined by the ability to remain balanced (or regain balance) during or after an action. There are several types of balance. (*See page 65.*)

Rhythm skills are defined as being able to synchronize one's own rhythm with that of another. This skill includes the ability to adapt to different kinds of equipment, such as a bicycle or, in our case, a horse. Ears, eyes and motion sensors are essential for rhythm skills.

Spatial orientation skills are defined as understanding the relationship between body and environment and adapting well to the perimeters of a defined space, such as performing in a dressage arena or on a jump course. The eye is the main collector and evaluator of information for spatial orientation.

Kinesthetic judgment skills are the skills needed to become aware of motions and sensations inside our own bodies using our five senses of smell, touch, sight, hearing and taste. Each sense is an analyzer, collecting information and making decisions based on the information. The more in tune we are with this, the more exactly and efficiently we can move. Spatial perception and awareness of the effect of various strengths/powers during a motion is foundational to gross motor skills as well as to finer motor skills, such as motions of the feet, hands, or head. These skills, combined with balancing skills and rhythm skills, are particularly important in horseback riding, since no situation feels or is the same, especially when riding a different horse.

Reaction skills are the ability to perform a specific action in response to predicted or unpredicted stimuli. A rider must always be on the alert in case the horse decides to suddenly change direction, halt, jump sideways or buck.

Influences on Coordination of Motion
Coordination of motion occurs when many smaller actions are linked together in order to reach a goal of a larger action. Each smaller, or partial, action is synchronized with the others to form the entire desired action. Many forces, both external and internal, influence coordination of motion and can cause certain problems. The following aspects are examples of such forces:

- The degree of freedom of motion needed to control one's body. In other words, to what degree can either horse or rider use his joints. It will be harder to coordinate the many smaller motions needed to bring the horse's hind legs under his body if the horse has arthritis in the hock joint, or even just poor conformation of the hock. It will be impossible for the rider to swing with the horse's motion if his ilio-sacral joint is blocked.
- Various strong external forces, such as air resistance, water resistance or hard soil resistance. It is much easier for the horse to coordinate his legs and body into an extended trot in good footing than in deep footing. The deep footing impedes the horse's ability to smoothly coordinate all the smaller motions in his body that are required to perform that extension. It is also easier for the rider to coordinate her body and aids when the footing is even than when it is inconsistent or a struggle for the horse. Any external force that influences either horse or rider will indirectly influence the other partner.
- Changes in a situation often caused by external influences on rider and horse (noises, slippery footing, rain, wind, audience). These influences often affect the mind of horse or rider, making it hard for the mind to coordinate the necessary motions and then to "let go" and allow them to happen. If the rider has performance anxiety, this will tend to show up in less coordinated bodily motions when riding.

AGILITY
Agility is defined as the ability to perform an action with quickness, lightness, ease of movement and full range of motion. The terms "suppleness," "elasticity," and "flexibility" fall under the term "agility." One's muscles must have an optimal range of motion, and one's joints must be able to support this range of motion. The range of muscle contraction determines one's dynamic range of motion. Agility has other forms as well:

General agility is defined as well-developed motion abilities in the shoulders, hips or spine. This is a good enough term for every day use for recreational riders. However, there is a difference between this kind of general agility and that of trained agility.

Specific agility refers to particular joints. A gymnast needs more flexibility in her joints than a swimmer does, for example. Ankles, knees, hips and shoulders are the most important joints for riders, whose motions involve the entire body, and must be flexible in order to adjust to the horse.

Active agility refers to the range of motion of a joint that, while flexing, also improves the suppleness of the extensor muscles. For example, the range of motion of the knee joint is affected by the suppleness of the hamstrings and the extending ability of the quadriceps. The interaction of all of these determines where a rider's knee falls. If the knee is high, the hamstrings and quadriceps may need some lengthening.

Passive agility is motion resulting from action somewhere else in the body. In the above example, passive agility would refer to the flexibility seen in the rider's ankle as a result of the interaction between the knee joint, the hamstrings, and the quadriceps. In general, people usually have better passive agility than active agility.

Anticipation of Motion

Anticipation of motion is defined as knowing the processes involved in a particular motion as well as having a clear picture of the end result in advance. Both the process of the motion and the result are predetermined before the action takes place because the athlete's subconscious already knows how the action will look.

A show jumping rider, for example, must foresee that during a 3-jump combination the horse must find the correct take off and landing over the first jump or else the distances for the remaining two jumps will be too difficult. Knowing this, if the horse takes off with too big an effort over the first fence, the rider must hold his horse back quickly in order to compensate and be able to clear the second and third fences. Riders must anticipate this situation and react accordingly. There is not time for the left brain to think through what needs to be done; instead, the right brain must instinctively react in the moment. This is known as "having a good eye."

How well riders can anticipate motions depends on their general motion experience. Riders with a sensitive feel can easily adapt themselves to their horse's motions when they have experience with a wide range of motions, understanding the inner processes that lead to the correct end results.

- A novice show jumping rider does not yet have enough experience with the motions required for jumping to be able to anticipate the correct striding and help the horse to find it. His lack of experience leads to unsure motions, which can confuse a horse who is also not sure of himself over jumps. The rider's motions are not yet in tune with those of the horse. This is why it is important for a novice rider to learn from an experienced horse, and vice versa.
- A dressage rider must anticipate the process of moving from a trot to a halt at a certain place in the arena so that she can use her half-halts appropriately to get the desired end result.

The General Basic Structure of Athletic Motions

Each motion of a horse and rider can be broken down into a three-phase structure. The three phases are preparation, main and end phase.

1-Preparation Phase

The preparation phase is important because it sets the rider up for a successful and on-target performance. It also prepares the rider for the main phase. The preparation phase in jumping, for example, is when a horse sinks down on his haunches while braking with his forehand. He saves energy this way, and is ready to propel himself over the jump. A dressage rider prepares her horse for an extension by asking for a little bit of over collection, to make sure that the horse's hind legs are well under his body and he is engaged and ready to push off into the extension. Without this preparation, the request for an extension would likely turn into the horse simply running faster on his forehand.

2-Main Phase

In this phase, a "solution" should be found to the "question" at hand. For a jumping horse the question is, "How do I get myself and my rider over the obstacle in front of us?" The solution is for him to rise up with his forehand and jump over the fence. Depending on the thoroughness of the preparation phase, this can either be successful or less successful. Failure to clear the fence is often caused by a problem in the preparation phase. The question asked of the dressage horse in the above example is, "What do I do with this additional energy that the rider is adding to the system?" With proper preparation, the solution is to move into an extended gait.

3-End Phase
In the end phase the dynamic climax leads to the reestablishment of balance or the motion is brought to completion. For a jumping horse this is the bascule. As the horse lands on the other side of the jump, the tendons in his front legs act as a cushion or shock absorber, and he brings his haunches underneath himself to rebalance himself for the next canter stride. At the end of the lengthened gait, the dressage horse must also coordinate his body to remain balanced while shortening the strides and continuing on in a working or collected gait.

Cyclical and Non-Cyclical Motions

Motions can be divided into two categories of motion, cyclical and non-cyclical. These categories describe the type of motion and whether it is repetitive and ongoing or whether it is a separate sequence inserted into an ongoing repetitive motion. These categories have significance for the rider because the use of aids may be different during cyclical and non-cyclical motions.

CYCLICAL MOTIONS
These are sequences of events that repeat themselves many times before the sequence is finished and the goal is accomplished, as in trotting or cantering. Instead of having preparation and end phases, we have a middle phase connecting each main phase to the next main phase. While trotting, a horse catches his weight on the landing by sinking a little with his joints. This small sinking motion is immediately followed by a new stretching motion, which suspends the horse in the air (moment of suspension). The same happens in a canter. After the three-beats the horse loses contact with the ground and lands again with his rear outer leg. Then the three-beat motion happens again.

In this cyclical sequence of motion the three phases are not clearly separated. The end phase (the sinking motion in a trot and canter) flows over into the preparation phase for the next stretching motion (the main phase), where the horse is momentarily suspended above the ground. End phases and preparation phases melt into each other. Riders can experience this in the trot when they either post the trot or sit the trot. The rider's body moves in a cyclical fashion as it moves in harmony with the horse's cyclical motion, by either posting up and down with each stride or by swinging the hips in the sitting trot.

A "running" trot or canter results when the phases do not smoothly flow into each other. For various reasons these horses cannot anticipate the ground very well. They fail to land softly and to transfer their weight from the landing to the new motion forward. When this occurs and the rider feels it in her seat, the rider must respond with her own cyclical motions of adjustment, pushing the horse forward with her legs, holding momentarily with seat and reins, and then releasing, in an attempt to help the horse rebalance and flow more smoothly forward.

NON-CYCLICAL MOTIONS

In non-cyclical motions, once the three-phases have ended, the motion is finished and the horse and rider can prepare for a different motion. The three phases of a jump, for example, are easy to identify: (1) the horse sinks on his haunches (preparation phase), then (2) the horse stretches up over the fence (main phase), and (3) there is a corresponding balance of horse and rider after landing (end phase). Each phase appears only once during the sequence of motions. A dressage horse traveling around the corner follows a non-cyclical pattern as well: (1) the rider prepares the horse for the corner by flexing the horse to the inside and beginning to ask the horse to bend in that direction (preparation phase), (2) the horse travels through the corner correctly bent for the depth of corner asked for by the rider (main phase), and (3) the rider straightens the horse as they come out of the corner and continue down the long side of the arena (end phase).

Combining Motions

Motions in riding are very rarely separate, or done in a way that they only affect one part of horse's and rider's bodies. Most motions are combinations of other motions, either within the horse, within the rider, or between the two. Motion combination involves the overall form of horse and rider, the connection between the partial motions of each, and their teamwork. Their entire muscle systems are at work even if the muscles that are working cannot be seen. The four most important points for successfully combining motions are the following:

- Using the torso correctly
- Flexing and straightening
- Twisting
- Using the head as the steering mechanism

USING THE TORSO CORRECTLY

The torso (or trunk of the body) is the largest mass in both horse and rider. It governs how they work as a team. The use of the torso can be broken down into two main categories:

Vertical, Horizontal and Sideways (right and left motion)

The rider's torso functions as a link between the rider's legs and the horse's trunk. In a trot these two forces either have a positive (supple) or negative (stiff) effect on each other. Stiff motions are caused by blockages in a rider's body, which hinder the smooth flow of the horse's motions vertically through the rider's body. Further disturbances occur when the rider's seat moves from side to side and up and down, again caused by blockages in a rider's body. If the rider's seat pounds against the horse's backbone, the horse will have more difficulty moving comfortably.

Rotation

Rotation of the torso requires flexing and bending the upper body. The rotation of the upper body should not be initiated by turning the upper body, but rather by turning the head. The head follows the direction of the eyes. The eyes direct the motions of the entire body. This is especially apparent when riding a circle, or when riding a movement that requires the horse to bend. Often riders will collapse their torsos to one side or the other rather than rotating the upper body correctly. Reminding the rider to initiate any movement in the torso with their eyes and heads will help prevent this problem.

— EXERCISES —

Dynamic Turning on the Long Axis

Of all the animals only humans are capable of turning on their long axis. This turning motion, however, has become more and more difficult for people in today's society. The result of not exercising this ability is a chain of tension in the body. Practicing this turning capability should be used frequently to remind the body of its wide range of motion possibilities.

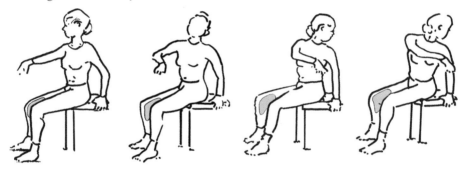

Fig. 1

Starting Position: Hold your arm out at shoulder level, with elbow bent, and hand hanging limp at the wrist about a foot in front of your eyes. Let your gaze follow your hand.

Movement: Begin in the center of your body and turn as far back behind you as possible, continuing to gaze at your hand. This should be done gently without force. If muscular tension does occur, you should not attempt to work any further. You should feel an extension in your range of motion with each repetition. Your body will quickly gain suppleness. Do this on both sides with each arm. After a few repetitions you will be able to look much farther behind you than in the beginning.

FLEXING AND STRAIGHTENING

This sequence of motions is found in posting trot, sitting trot, and jumping. In posting trot and in sitting trot the rider's body is constantly getting taller and then shorter. This motion is more obvious in posting trot as the rider physically comes out of the saddle in rhythm with the horse's trot. In order for the rider to stay in balance with the horse through this motion the upper body must flex and straighten appropriately. In the sitting trot, the motion is not as obvious, but the rider's body still has to flex and straighten in order to absorb the motion of the horse's trot. The spine and joints must be flexible and the muscles must be supple enough to allow this sequence. This straightening up (tall) and flexing (short) motion can be hindered by various blockages.

TWISTING

A fluidly seated rider has his shoulders and hips parallel to the shoulders and hips of his horse at all times (Fig. 2). Thus, much of the time he sits twisted, meaning that his shoulder axis is turned into his hip axis.

Every time the horse bends his body, this corresponding motion of the rider must occur in order for the rider and horse to remain in harmony. When appropriate twisting does not occur, the rider turns "like a bus," laterally, with the shoulders remaining parallel to the hips (an "open seat") and may collapse one hip or side of the body. Many riders have trouble coordinating the correct posture because they cannot perform the required cross-coordination movements (*see Cross Coordination page 60*).

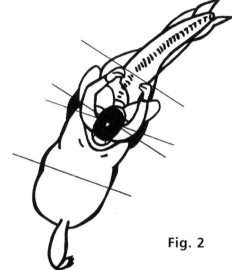

Fig. 2

USING THE HEAD AS THE STEERING MECHANISM

Motions of the head directly affect the spine, which in turn affects body position and posture, either in a positive or negative way. For example, when you lower your chin, your spine makes a C-form, and when you raise your chin high up in the air, your spine automatically curves the other way. The same applies when riding. If the rider's head is too low, they have a round back; when the head is thrown back too far, they have a hollow back. Horses exhibit the same response. If the horse puts his head down, his spine curves upward, and when he throws his head in the air, his back hollows. If a horse holds his head crooked, he will not be able to walk straight. The horse pulls on the reins and cannot swing in his gait like he should because the back is blocked.

Characteristics of Motion

All motions have certain characteristics that are important to pay attention to in evaluating and teaching a horse and rider. With experience and training people can learn to see these various characteristics of motion in horse and rider and can begin to judge the quality of a performance based on these characteristics rather than simply looking at whether horse and rider fit a pre-defined form. Being able to see motions is important, but being able to feel them is even more important, because it is at the level of feel that changes can be made. Riders must feel the motions of their own bodies and their horses' bodies before being able to make changes to those motions.

STRENGTH OF MOTION — Power

Strength of motion describes the degree of strength needed for completing a motion or action. The use of more strength and more force does not necessarily lead to a better outcome. For example, too much force of hand or too much thumping of the legs does not help produce the desired motion; instead it hinders the production of this motion. The use of power in all parts of the body must be balanced. Forward driving aids must be coordinated with the appropriate balancing rein aids. Too much power in the leg muscles while driving a horse causes him to react too vigorously. Applying different levels of strength with the aids produces other reactions as well, such as changes in tempo (medium trot to extended trot) or direction. In an extended trot a horse's motions are not any quicker, but his strides are simply farther apart. In a half-pass, the horse's rhythm and tempo stay the same, but his direction of travel changes.

CADENCE OF MOTION — Speed

If the cadence is too quick in relation to the general ability of a horse, the entire motion of horse and rider can be thrown out of tune (for example, the trot becomes jarring and the rider's legs slap against the horse's sides). In a posting trot the rider must match his rhythm to that of the horse. If this does not happen the rider will rush the horse or disrupt his cadence. A lack of cadence is often the visible manifestation of a deficiency in another area, for example in rhythm. A horse who does not have a solid rhythm with looseness will rush faster with a tight back when asked for longer strides. A rider who does not have a solid sense of rhythm will often throw the horse out of balance, causing the horse to react by rushing forward or stopping.

RANGE OF MOTION — Spatial Expansion

Spatial expansion is defined as range of motion. A horse's range of motion is larger in an extended canter than in a medium canter, which, in turn, is larger than in a collected canter.

Some of a rider's aids can be made ineffective by a range of motion that is inappropriate for the situation. If the rider's legs flop against the horse's sides too actively, they will disrupt the task that the horse is performing. If a rider loses her reins as she approaches a jump, this sudden increase in the horse's range of motion may result in a problem at that jump (refusal or rail down). Many riders post too high in the posting trot, but when the rider's range of motion is too large here the horse's pace, rhythm and entire flow of motion can suffer.

RHYTHM OF MOTION — Time Sequencing

Rhythm of motion is part of the structural aspect of motion because it expresses the distinctive time sequencing of a motion, building upon a basic structure.

This detailed look at the structure of a motion involves the timing of the partial processes, which are connected during the entire motion process. A trot or walk cadence, for example, is attained with the exact timing of each step. Regulation of the time sequence, however, touches on only one aspect of rhythm—the beat; whereas rhythm, in its entirety, possesses an additional spatial and energetic component. Rhythm is based on the balanced use of all muscle groups.

It is fairly easy for a person to understand rhythmic motion through audio and visual stimuli. These stimuli have a contagious effect. An observer actually tenses his muscles (often not visibly) and even sometimes moves with the performer as though he were performing the action himself. This means that a person who already knows a move by heart automatically completes the move internally when he carefully observes another person performing it. During such an observation the same bio-chemical processes occur inside the observer as they do inside the performer.

Rhythm is divided into natural rhythm and ridden rhythm. The horse initially provides the rider with a **natural rhythm** based on the horse's individual characteristics (size, strength, level of training, personality). The rider must adapt himself to the horse's natural rhythm to facilitate harmonious teamwork. Only when a rider's rhythm is identical with that of his horse can he begin to influence and change the horse's rhythm with his body **(ridden rhythm)** and teach the horse specific movements necessary for the desired type and level of riding. The ideal rhythm between horse and rider can be observed as a smooth and flowing motion within each gait as well as from one gait to the next, or one movement to the next.

This process of becoming an effective team of horse and rider is extremely complex, and difficulties are common. Not every rider, no matter how skilled, can be expected to work well with every horse. Not every horse is "his" horse. Each horse and rider combines many physical actions, and thus, many rhythms, timings, and sequences. The more complete this combining process is between horse and rider, the more polished and unique is their rhythmical motion.

CONSISTENCY OF MOTION — Identical Repetition

Well-schooled horses show great consistency in the length and frequency of their strides. Consistency of motion is defined as the ongoing degree of harmony between horse and rider in each phase of the motion structure (preparation, main, and end phases). We differentiate between *regularity of accomplishment (*a jumper clearing a fence without a problem) and *regularity of quality* (performance consistency, such as a dressage horse performing an excellent flying lead change). In many situations, both regularities are required and subsequently depend on one another to function. For example, the dressage horse performing the flying change must have regularity of *accomplishment* in being able to correctly execute the flying change when asked, and only then can begin to work towards regularity of *quality*, by adding impulsion, precision and expressiveness to the flying changes to make them excellent.

PRECISION OF MOTION — Agreement Between Plan and Result
Precision of motion occurs when the planned motion coincides with the performed motion. The degree of harmony between these two motions (planned and performed) is important. In other words, how well the actual performance turns out in relation to the planned performance determines the precision of motion. Examples of precision of motion include: a flying lead change at a chosen point in the arena, finding the right take-off spot for a jump, coming to a complete halt at a specific letter, backing up a pre-determined number of steps, or completing a cross-country course in exactly the optimum time.

Analysis of Motion as Seen From the Outside

This section applied the morphological approach, which comes from the study of motion, to the scientific study of riding motions. This approach attempts to dig deeper into the sources of deviations by dealing with the individual ability of each rider. This can eventually help riding instructors observe and judge their students more effectively. Students and instructors must get used to analyzing motions, not only subjectively, but objectively. This system of analysis allows all participants to see a performance with the same "glasses." Riding instructors are often expected to be able to perform all riding actions flawlessly in order to be a good example to their students. At the same time, they must know and be able to recognize the correct sequence of motions in a performance. If they are not aware of this, they cannot impart the correct image of a motion to their students (audibly or visually).

If instructors have a correct image of the motion in their head and can talk with their students about the mental aspects of performing that motion, they can recognize mistakes more quickly and precisely. They can also choose the best method to use to correct a mistake, taking into account their student's abilities. In order to judge the quality of an action correctly, instructors must judge according to certain established criteria, and these criteria must first be discussed with the student so that the student knows what is expected and why.

Analysis of Motion as Seen From the Inside – Balance and Motion

Effective riding is made up of balance and motion, or more precisely balance *in* motion. Balance cannot occur without motion and motion cannot occur without balance. This equation holds true throughout most of life; even walking from one place to another requires both balance and motion. For riders, though, these variables are even more important because of the presence of the horse, which has its own balance and motion to coordinate. All of these motions and balance abilities must come together in order to achieve success in riding.

> *Balance cannot occur without motion and motion cannot occur without balance.*

The following concepts influence motion and our understanding of it. Every rider and instructor usually learns about the horse's motions, beginning with the basic understanding of the three gaits and moving into a deeper and more complicated understanding of the biomechanics of the horse's various motions while being ridden. Riders and instructors may not, however, follow the same procedure of developing an understanding of the biomechanics of the rider's motions. The following underlying principles will help you better understand motion in both horse and human.

WHAT IS APPLIED KINESIOLOGY?

The term "kinesiology" comes from the Greek term "kinesis" which means motion. "Applied kinesiology" is the science of studying body motions. Kinesiology is a multidisciplinary science encompassing three primary areas of study. These areas are Biomechanics, Exercise Physiology, and Psychomotor Behavior. Kinesiologists use these three primary sciences to study human movement. It is a holistic approach which attempts to keep motion and the interaction between energy systems in the human body balanced. Instructors and students should be aware that this field is very wide and deep. In the United States many types of kinesiology have been intensely studied and practiced for years. It stems originally from chiropractics and, today, is also applied to and supplements many various medical disciplines.

A key part of applied kinesiology is its use in the instructional process of teaching/coaching physical activity and sports. Learning and teaching methods using theories from applied kinesiology are very different from traditional methods. It offers a different perspective on how people learn motion. There are other forms of kinesiology that study muscles and how to test and balance them to maintain and regain psychological and electro-magnetic balance. Traditional kinesiology is simply tapping into the information that our minds and bodies have stored in our muscles and using this information for preventive and therapeutic purposes.

The applicability of kinesiology to horseback riding is high, but more work needs to be done to determine specifically how this is to be accomplished and what it will look like. Since horseback riding involves learning motion and improving performance, the opportunities to learn from the field of kinesiology are many. Unfortunately, many instructors are not aware of the numerous and subtle factors in a learning environment that can cause harmful effects on their students. These negative factors have a direct effect on the psychological and electro-magnetic energies in our bodies.

For the purposes of this book I have incorporated principles of applied kinesiology into the exercises described throughout the book as well as in the assessment of deviations students often make while learning to ride. The Instructor Section is dedicated to teaching skills and suggestions that also incorporate kinesthetic wisdom. The rather short discourse here about applied kinesiology is only meant to give the reader a general idea about this very complex and intricate field. I have tried to lay a foundation for the application of kinesiology to riding lessons. In brief, students must learn to balance using their entire body, with the help of specific exercises. They must also be able to be in motion such that their psychological and electromagnetic energies stay balanced.

Sensitive Learning and Applied Kinesiology

Coaching colleges should expand their horizons by including applied kinesiology in their programs. The application of kinesiology to horseback riding needs to be further researched and developed, just as "exercise programs" for the brain need to be further developed for horseback riding. I strongly encourage instructors and students to research this topic themselves and find out more about it. Seminars or conferences about kinesiology are excellent ways to become

---

THE DISCIPLINE

Kinesiology (from the Greek words "KINEIN", to move, and "LOGOS", to study) is the scientific study of movement. The primary aims of Kinesiology are:

- *understanding the human body's physiological and psychological responses to acute short-term physical activity,*

- *understanding the various adaptations of the human body to chronic or long-term physical activity,*

- *understanding the cultural, social, and historical importance of physical activity,*

- *understanding the mechanical qualities of movement,*

- *understanding the processes that control movement and the factors that affect the acquisition of motor skills, and*

- *understanding the psychological effects of physical activity on human behavior.*

To achieve these aims, research in Kinesiology requires the use of a variety of scientific knowledge and research techniques from such fields as biology, chemistry, history, physics, psychology, and sociology. The areas of investigation within Kinesiology are quite extensive because the responses of the human body to physical activity can be examined at many levels (from cellular to whole society).

more familiar with the material and be able to apply it to practical circumstances.

INNER/OUTER MATCHING

Many riders tend to have a different picture of themselves from that which observers see. They have not learned to see themselves correctly from within. Riders must learn to look inside themselves before they can begin to learn to feel motion. It is very interesting that the riders who know their bodies the best and know how to see inside themselves are the best riders overall. Weaker riders usually have a better picture of themselves (and their motions) in their head than what their actual motions are. Stronger riders know both their strengths and their weaknesses, and do not overly focus on either one. They know how to make the most of their strengths and work to improve their weaknesses, without negative thinking or worry.

Additionally, instructors and riders need to learn to see the whole picture so as to be able to determine where the root of a deviation may lie. It is not enough for the instructor to look at the rider's hands bouncing around and tell the rider to keep his hands quiet. She needs to use her "inner eye," the ability to "feel" what the rider is feeling, to determine what might be the inner cause of the rider's bouncing hands. Is there tension in the pelvis or neck that is being transferred through the rider's body and is appearing in the hands? Is the rider fearful and holding onto the reins too tightly, causing the bouncing? There are many possible underlying reasons for a visible deviation from the rider's individual ideal, and effective instruction is instruction that goes to the root cause rather than focusing on the visible result. Once riders begin to understand this concept, they can work with the instructor to find that root cause. Riders may experiment with motions in different parts of their bodies to see how it affects an identified deviation. Riders who are able to do this take a more active role in their own learning, and become much more effective riders and learners. They also experience less frustration because they understand that finding their own ideal position is not simply a matter of willpower, but involves trial and error throughout their whole bodies.

— EXERCISES FOR LEARNING MOTIONS —

Cross-coordination Motions

Movements: This exercise is done in an alternating rhythm. Opposing limbs are moved together (right arm and left leg; left arm and right leg). You should move forward, backward and to the side. Your eyes should follow the motion of your body. Move your right (or left) hand to the opposing knee at least 3 times, crossing the body's centerline (down the middle). Crossing the centerline can also be done with opposing hands and feet behind your back. This can be done in the form of walking, skipping or crawling.

Although you can use various levels of effort, be careful not to overexert yourself; otherwise muscle cramps will result. This exercise can also be done in slow motion and with the arms and legs partially or fully stretched. When switching sides you can hop lightly or bounce from one foot to the other. It can also be done while sitting, with your eyes closed and with appropriate music.

Results:

- increases eye movement to the right and to the left
- improves two-eyed 3D vision, left-right-coordination, spatial orientation, hearing and vision (in general)
- aids breathing and general fitness

Fig. 3

Sideways Figure Eights

Starting Position: Gaze into the air in front of you at eye level. This point is the middle of the figure eight. Hold one arm straight out in front of you at this level.

Movements: In a relaxed posture use your thumb or forefinger to draw sideways figure eights in the air. You should determine the height and width of these figures yourself. However, it is most effective when your figure eights are large, requiring full range of motion in the arms and encompassing the entire peripheral vision field. Starting in the middle of the body at eye level move your arm upwards and in a counter-clockwise direction, making a circle and then returning to the middle point. After crossing the middle point move clockwise upwards and to the right making a circle and returning to the middle point. Do this at least three times.

This exercise is very relaxing and centering when done with closed eyes. Humming can also enhance this exercise, although the head (and eyes) should begin following the movement after a while to relax the neck.

Results:

- combines the use of the left and right sides of the brain
- improves spatial, 3D and peripheral vision, eye motion ability and coordination
- relaxes the eyes, neck and shoulders by crossing over the body's center line

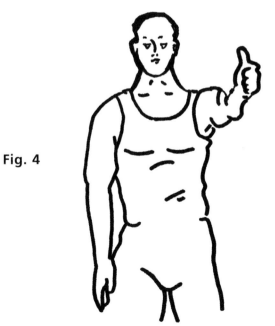

Fig. 4

The Elephant

Starting position: Lean your head on one shoulder with both eyes open. Extend your arm on that side and gaze along your arm into space.

Movements: Your hand, arm, head and chest should all move as one and draw sideways figure eights in the air (see Figure 5). Your gaze should be focused just beyond your hand.

This exercise can also be done in a sitting position. Make varying wide range motions (right-left; up-down) with your "elephant trunk." Using a wide range of motion is very important. After a while you can switch arms.

Test: Before and after this exercise instructors should ask their students to check how relaxed (or tight) their neck and shoulders are by moving their head from side to side and front and back.

Results:

- incorporates the senses of sight and hearing with the motion of the entire body
- crosses over the centerline, enhancing cross-coordination abilities
- increases the range of motion from right to left
- relaxes the neck by focusing
- increases spatial, 3D vision, balance (stimulates the inner ear and other balancing organs), and coordination between upper and lower body (transfer of motion)

Fig. 5

Summary

The abilities described above can only be developed when the right conditions during childhood exist. In general, children need a stimulating and active environment, so that they can completely make use of all of their genetic predispositions. A newborn's central reflexes react directly to the stimuli in his environment, for example the important grip-reflex and the neck reflex.

The grip-reflex refers to how newborns can close their fingers around small objects, such as an adult's finger. This reflex is important for the development of specific grips later on, such as holding the reins. The neck reflex refers to how stronger babies always raise their heads when turned on their stomachs. It is an important developmental step towards being able to sit up straight and learning to walk upright.

Many riders in more recent generations have problems performing rhythmical and specific motions with the reins and also have trouble holding their heads upright. These problems could have originated from a lack of infant development during the phases mentioned above. If parents or caregivers are not educated about the importance of these reflexes problems can arise later on. Riders and instructors need to be aware of these developmental milestones because it can help explain blockages that some riders may encounter during their learning process. There are exercises that riders can do to help "catch up" in any areas that they may have skipped over during childhood.

Riding as a Game of Balance

Balance is a term with many applications in riding. It can refer to simple physical balance of the rider herself (i.e. can she stand on her own two feet on the ground, with even weight on both sides, without falling down?), to the balance of the horse (longitudinal or lateral), to the balance of the horse and the rider together (are they in harmony?), to the balance of various muscles in the horse's and rider's bodies (i.e. a horse may have an overdeveloped muscle on the underside of his neck, making it hard for him to stretch into the rider's contact; or a rider may have overdeveloped inner thigh muscles from aerobics classes), to mental balance (i.e. the ability to think clearly and calmly in a variety of situations), and more! Balance is really a way of approaching a situation, keeping an open mind and seeking to see and feel both sides of any issues as well as both sides of your body. All forms of balance are important in achieving success in riding; you must find a balance between all of the types of balance! We will define several of them here. You will find many exercises throughout this book related to creating balance in horse, rider, and instructor.

Physical Balance

Staying balanced on a horse is not like anything else, although surfing and skiing are the sports most similar to horseback riding. They, too, require years of practice, enormous effort and intense concentration. Horseback riding is even more complicated than surfing or skiing because instead of standing on an inactive object (like a surfboard or skis) riders sit on a live, moving creature that has a will of its own! Things also happen much faster and are much more complex than in other sports. Riders cannot make analogies to any other sports to help them while riding. Riding is simply a very unique and very challenging experience that can also be very rewarding.

Balancing skills refer to the ability to remain balanced (or regain balance) during or after a motion. Balance is never static; it is always dynamic. It can never be achieved once and for all, but is always having to be regained. There are several types of balance that are useful to understand: 1) upright balance, 2) balance while moving from one place to another, 3) rotational or turning balance, and 4) balance in the air. Upright balance is defined as being able to *remain balanced* or regain balance while standing still, either on the ground or while sitting on a horse that is not moving. Even when we think that we are standing absolutely still, we are actually making many small internal motions to be able to remain in that upright balance. Essentially this is balance in one dimension. Balance while moving from one place to another is the balance that results when you create a disturbance from upright balance and so must regain balance. When you take a step forward you put yourself off balance and must make many inner and outer adjustments to regain your balance. This type of balance also applies to riding a moving horse. The horse is creating the disturbance from your natural upright balance and you must figure out what you need to do to remain balanced on the back of the horse as he moves forward or backward. This is balance in two dimensions. Rotation balance adds a third dimension, which is turning. Not only do riders have to maintain their upright balance and regain their balance when the horse is in motion, but also have to make adjustments to regain balance lost when the horse changes direction. Balance in the air is applicable when riding any gait where there is a moment of suspension. At this moment there is no contact with the ground and both horse and rider must adjust their bodies in order to regain balance lost due to this loss of contact with the ground. This is most obvious when a horse is jumping over obstacles, but is also present in the trot and canter.

There are three functions of the human body that are used for every kind of balancing skill: 1) the vestibular system in the inner ear, 2) sensors in the skin, and 3) motion sensors (kinesthetic analysis).

Beginner or novice riders usually try to stay on their horse using any means possible. They grab on with their legs and try to counteract any motion the horse makes, often by pulling on the reins. These abrupt and rough movements actually make the situation worse because the horse may react by either speeding up or bucking to get away from its bothersome rider.

The key for beginners is to realize that they must find their balance in an entirely different way than they are accustomed to. Instead of clamping their legs on to the horse, they must relax their legs, free their pelvis and use the stomach muscles to stabilize the body. Relaxed muscles react much faster than tensed muscles. Tensed muscles must first relax before they can react to commands from the brain. Therefore, if a person's muscles are already relaxed and "ready," his or her reactions will be much quicker. Thus, a rider who is concerned about being in control of the horse needs to learn that she is actually more in control with relaxed muscles than with tense muscles, even though it may not feel that way. In order to stay balanced riders must constantly be in motion; that is, their muscles are constantly reacting to changes in the horse. A rider who tries to remain absolutely still will not be balanced. Riders must constantly regain balance, which means that their brain is constantly sending signals to their muscles. Therefore, the more relaxed their muscles are the better they will be able to balance. The same principle applies to people standing on the ground. When we are standing "still" we are actually making lots of tiny adjustments and motions with our various muscles to hold our bodies upright.

Sitting in the saddle is not at all like sitting in a chair. Horseback riders do not sit "on" something, but rather they sit balanced *with* the horse. Riders need to find their own balance in the saddle so that they can assist the horse in finding his balance beneath them. Horses have a natural balance when running free in the pasture, but this balance is significantly altered when a rider is put on their back. People can feel this when they give piggy-back rides to small children. Every move that the child makes results in an adjustment of the person's own balance in order to stay upright. Riders also must constantly deal with changes in their center of gravity, which are caused by the motion of the horse and changes in the horse's rhythm. The best way to stay balanced is to become one with the horse and take on his rhythm and motion. To do so, riders must have a dynamic seat, not a stationary one.

Later I will discuss some specific lessons that help both rider and horse with their balance. Developing balance together means communicating with each other constantly; it means having an ongoing dialogue between a rider's pelvis and the horse's back.

Balanced Muscles

Unfortunately, every rider has muscular imbalances. These imbalances are the root of riders' deviations from the ideal position and use of the aids. Day-to-day activities (housework, for example), bad posture at the work place, incorrect lifting or carrying, over exertion and not enough or incorrect physical activity puts uneven strain on both sides of the body. This restricts the range of motion in those muscles that are already prone to shorten. Inactivity, forgetting to exercise certain muscle groups or doing incorrect exercises make weak muscles even weaker, so that they cannot counterbalance the muscles that are too strong. To help prevent and also to repair what damage has already been done, it is of utmost importance to *stretch* the muscles which tend to shorten and to *strengthen* the muscles that tend to be weak. If this simple principle is followed riders can avoid incorrect posture and improve their overall position in the saddle. (See *Exercise Program for Riders,* Meyners 2003)

STRETCHING (to achieve optimal muscle length— for shortened, over-used muscles)

There are two main types of stretching; springy stretching, which uses movement within the stretch, and "held muscle extension," where the stretch is held without movement for a period of time. Springy stretching activates the body's naturally occurring protective reflex mechanism, the anti-stretching reflex, which resists tension and prevents tearing or damage to the muscles. While use of these exercises optimally prepares muscles for the stresses that will be placed on them, it also prevents us from achieving our desired goals of lengthening because the muscle, fearing being torn, tightens against the stretch. For this reason, springy stretching alone will not lead to the optimal muscle length.

It is important to consider the strength of the muscles and to be sure that the sequence of loads corresponds with the current muscle capacity. *If a muscle has its optimal length, it is also maximally efficient.* This is why stretching practices are important preparation for the strengthening practices that will follow. An additional benefit of stretching is the increased temperature of the musculature.

A muscle can be injured if there is insufficient preparation followed by a strong springy action. The brain does not stimulate the signal for the muscle to relax so it remains tight and does not stretch. If you first get the muscle to relax, then the muscle can be optimally stretched. In this moment of automatic relaxation, the muscle can be stretched very effectively.

"Held muscle extension" results in an optimal extension of the muscle. This is achieved if the muscle is carefully stretched and held for approximately ten seconds. After this time, the brain will give the command to the anti-stretching reflex to relax. This moment must be used for further stretching of the muscle. The following is one method to use to achieve "held muscle extension" stretching. It is called the S-H-R-S-Method. "S" (starting position) designates the initial position where you become aware of where the muscle is tense. This is training perception in the muscle. Begin a gentle stretch of the tight area. "H" (hold) means that this position is supposed to be held for approximately ten seconds. After this time, the anti-stretching reflex automatically lets go and the muscle relaxes. "R" (relax) indicates the phase, about two seconds long (not longer), in which the muscle is relaxed. While this happens, however, the produced extension of the muscle must not be abandoned. This phase is only a short-term interruption of the stretch. "S" (stretch) means an additional stretching over the previously reached limit. This process of S-H-R-S can be repeated two to five times per muscle group.

Another effect of systematic stretching is that the muscle opposite the one being stretched becomes stronger. Thus it makes sense that correctly structured stretching is an effective method to build an ideal muscle balance in the body. These principles of stretching are important to keep in mind when performing the stretching/lengthening exercises at the end of this section (*see pages ......*).

> *When lengthening or strengthening muscles people can make mistakes that do not attain the goals originally intended by the exercise. Furthermore, they can eventually hinder that muscle's function. Daily exercises at home are helpful for effective training in order to deal with muscle weakness as quickly as possible. The best solution is to use these exercises at home two times per week in addition to regular riding lessons. You should also work on your personal "weak points" at home before riding.*

STRENGTHENING (to achieve optimal muscle length— for muscles that are too long or under-used)

All strengthening practices are to be performed either isometrically or very slowly. In fast strengthening movements, not all muscle fibers are addressed. Movements initiated with momentum reach only a part of the muscle and do not strengthen its full length. It is important to be aware of this process if each muscle is to reach its optimal function.

The person's respiration is also disturbed through abrupt strengthening practices. In the use of forced practices, the flow of air is strained and interrupted. Tension in the breathing process is injurious for healthy muscle building and can be damaging to the organs. A natural and consistent oxygen supply is necessary for the most efficient and healthy development of the body.

When the respiration is strained, a person's face will turn red. The person stops the air as it comes in and does not breathe deeply into the body. A large pressure results in the blood vessels, which can be easily seen in the veins of the neck as they become engorged with blood. This process results in dizziness or seeing black. In order to avoid this you must, in all practices, keep breathing in a steady, rhythmical way.

Each time that the breath is interrupted, the movement sequence will also become jerky, and the opposite is also true. If the movement is jerky, the breathing will also be jagged. The rider needs to become aware of his or her breath as well as the smoothness of his or her actions in the strengthening exercises. Pushing too hard or too long leads to sinking blood pressure and also to an oxygen deficiency in the body. This situation is automatically followed by a diminishment in performance.

Principles for strengthening practices: Each exercise should be repeated ten to fifteen times, as smoothly as possible. The repetition number can be increased according to the needs of the muscle.

In isometric strengthening, where you hold the exercise without moving, ten seconds holding time should be possible. The rider carefully moves into the position required by the exercise and then holds that position. This holding time can be increased according to the person's state of development (e.g. until thirty seconds). The person can also increase repetitions of the exercise, pausing for ten to twenty seconds after the first hold and then holding again. This can be repeated one or more times.

Using a combination of springy and held muscle extension stretching, followed by appropriate strengthening exercises, will lead to the balanced muscles necessary for the rider to learn and perform to the best of his ability. These principles of strengthening are important to keep in mind when using the strengthening exercises at the end of this section.

— EXERCISES FOR DEVELOPING BALANCE —

Once you have prepared your body using appropriate stretching and strengthening exercises, there are additional exercises you can do on the horse to improve the various aspects of balance that are necessary for successful riding.

Tongue to Teeth

Our tongues have a major influence on our body energy and balance. When a person is in a stressful situation, the tongue can be influencial in grounding them again. When the tongue is lightly pressed on the gums about ¼ inch behind the upper front teeth, the body's energy stabilizes and becomes centered. This simple technique, not visible to the outside observer, can be used very effectively in competition situations or any other time that the rider feels stress and tension.

This can be felt with an experiment on the ground. Ask a person to stand on one foot. Then pull on one arm to pull her off balance. This will probably be quite easy and not require much effort on your part. Ask her to lightly press her tongue against the top gum just behind her front teeth. When you try to pull her off balance this time, you will have to pull a lot harder, as she is better grounded and centered.

Changing Stirrup Length

Often riders choose a certain stirrup length and always ride with the stirrups at that "perfect" length. They may be afraid to change them for fear of disrupting their positions; or they just may not think about adjusting the stirrups. However, difficulties developing balance can arise if riders leave their stirrups the same length all the time. The motion of the rider becomes habitually the same and they lose their ability to feel and their sense of balance. If riders change their stirrup lengths more frequently, they challenge themselves and their horses to train under different balance conditions. The rider's center of gravity changes, requiring a wider range of balancing abilities. This will also help the rider to develop balancing skills that can be applied to a variety of horses since each horse has a unique motion which the rider must adapt to. These changes in stirrup length can be anywhere from one hole up or down to four, five, or more holes. Riders who approach this exercise with an open mind and ready for a challenge will find that they become much more secure and comfortable in the saddle, giving them more freedom of motion and increasing their options for responding to the horse's movements.

"Monkey Posture" (Two-point, Jumping Position)

The "monkey posture," so named by F.M. Alexander, the founder and developer of the Alexander Technique, is a posture of optimal relaxation and balance for the human body. Riders know this position as the "two-point" or "jumping position." It is a very effective way for riders to develop the correct balance, and can be paired with the exercise of varying the stirrup length for additional challenge and balance development. In the "monkey posture" the rider rises up out of the saddle and leans forward so that the shoulders are over the knees and the hips stay over the heels. The stirrups must be short enough that the rider's knees are bent and extend towards the front of the saddle flap. When the rider is in the correct position the lower legs are parallel to the rider's trunk. This position allows the rider to lengthen the spine. The ankles, knees, hips, and shoulders are all open in this position, which allows motion to flow through the rider's whole body. The hips act as a hinge (Fig. 7) and the head is then able to use its full range of motion.

This "monkey posture" helps alleviate stiffness in riders by allowing them to loosen up and free their joints. At first riders may

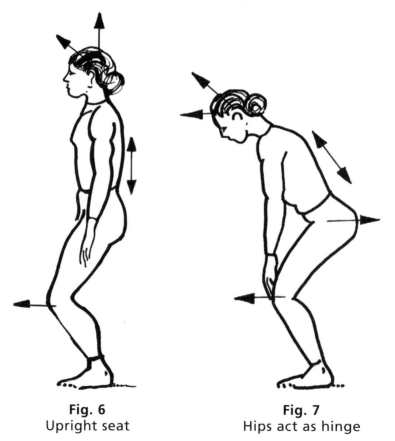

Fig. 6
Upright seat

Fig. 7
Hips act as hinge

hold their joints stiff, but as they become comfortable and aware of their joints, they will develop the ability to use the hip, knee, and ankle joints as "shock absorbers," moving with the horse's movement. This position educates the joints in the motion they need to allow in order to be in harmony with the horse, and the effects can be seen in the posting and sitting trot as well. This posture is not easy and must be practiced again and again. It can be used in all three gaits; walk, trot, and canter, as well as over cavalletti and jumps. The stirrups must be raised enough to allow the rider to open and close the joints in their ankles, knees, hips, and shoulders while practicing the position in each gait. Then, when the stirrups are made longer again riders who are normally too stiff will be much more relaxed, and riders who are usually too loose will have more correct, natural body tone.

Opposing Motions

The exercise of opposing motions asks the rider to sit in some exaggerated ways, such as leaning to the right and then to the left, or leaning forward and then backward. Riders can imagine that they are a blow up doll with a weight in the bottom, and somebody is pushing the top part in all directions, but when the pressure is released, the "doll" bounces back to the upright seated position. Practicing these motions can improve a rider's feel for the correct seat, and trains the body how to sit in a balanced but flexible manner on the horse's back. Finding the correct seat is not a simple task and does not happen instantaneously. Moving in different directions and trying different positions can help the brain filter out the positions that do not work. When the rider sits "normally" again, the brain and the senses will automatically find the correct seat that puts the rider in balance with the horse. This exercise is especially helpful for riders who sit too rigidly on the horse, or who have trouble harmonizing their balance with that of their horse.

Jumping Exercises

Jumping is a wonderful way to develop balance in a rider as riders must learn to sit in a balanced manner that allows the horse to negotiate the obstacle successfully and is comfortable for both horse and rider. Jumping exercises improve a rider's feel for motion and are important for riders of all disciplines. They are especially important for younger riders who, unfortunately, seem to specialize in one discipline much too early. Young riders who specialize too early will have trouble later on as their bodies will not develop all of the motion abilities necessary to ride a variety of horses in a variety of situations. Show jumping riders should constantly improve their balance with exercises in dressage, and dressage riders should integrate jumping exercises into their training activities to help improve their balance.

Here are a few sample tasks that can be used to test and develop a rider's balance: jumping several cavalletti in succession (as in a grid) first with reins, then without reins, and then without stirrups or reins. Riders should be required to have a wide range of balancing abilities and good communication skills with the horse.

Psychological and Mental Influences on Riding

Because riders are complex beings and not just bodies that can be commanded to act in a certain way, thoughts and emotions have a profound effect on a person's ability to learn. The power of the mind to influence the body is incredible, and we are only just now beginning to understand the depths of that communication. When a person has had a bad day, this will affect their ability to ride that day. It will also affect their ability to learn from instruction and to interact with their instructor and their horse. Through awareness riders can learn to use the power of their minds to overcome negative influences and to open themselves to new learning experiences, despite the challenges they may be facing, but this is a learned skill which is quite difficult. Instructors who are aware of this process can facilitate the development of this ability in riders through demonstration and education.

Awareness is the key "first step" in learning to effectively use the psychology of the mind to benefit riding and learning. Below are some examples of behaviors and thought processes to become aware of:

Having Fun Yet?

At riding competitions I often ask myself if riders are actually having fun. When I look at their faces I am astonished to see that many have grimaces and frowns on their faces. They do not look like they are having a good time. They look much too serious. Their expressions reveal a great deal about their inner emotions, and their entire body reflects their facial expressions. If they frown and grimace, their whole body tenses up, their shoulders hunch, their head sinks, and their back gets round. This can also be observed in daily riding sessions, even without the stress of competition. A stranger wandering into a barn and watching a lesson may wonder why the riders are putting themselves through this apparently unpleasant situation!

As we have learned, relaxed muscles function better (and more quickly) than tensed muscles. Even a little smile can have an effect on riders' muscles and allow them to smoothly undulate with the horse's rhythm. A smile moves through the rider's body and the horse feels this and relaxes. This relaxation promotes more effective communications between the two parties. This is the main reason that riding lessons should create a relaxed and fun atmosphere. Tense situations should be avoided as much as possible since a positive atmosphere facilitates success more than a negative atmosphere.

Concentration & Focus

Riders need to have flexibility of focus and concentration, being able to move between an inner awareness of their own body, their horse's body and the goal, and an outer awareness of what the instructor is saying and what is going on in the environment around them. Over-focusing, or focusing on one particular object and being "blind" to other stimuli, is a common rider problem. Riders generally tend to gaze in one particular direction. "Tunnel vision," which is often caused by an inner mental state of over-focusing, causes tension in the body. If riders have a tendency of looking rigidly straight in front of them, instructors should give them the task of looking a little to the right and to the left – to be more flexible with their gaze. It is amazing what positive effects this little task will have on the rider's seat. They are then able to move much more smoothly with the horse. This exercise can also be performed when riding a circle. People are taught to look to the center of the circle, or in the direction they are going, which is correct, but the gaze should not be fixed.

Having riders move their heads and eyes a little bit, while still looking generally in the direction in which they are traveling, will bring them much more in harmony with the horse.

Riders also tend to stare at the horse's head and neck, as if "willing" it to be in the correct position. This also has a negative effect on their seats. They tend to stick their head out, with the chin jutting forward, and the head then sinks down into their neck, blocking the occipital joint. When this joint is relaxed and "free," the whole body is also relaxed and "free." In order to "free" this joint, riders should practice looking forward and a little downward (Fig. 9). This can be accomplished by gazing at the ground between the horse's ears.

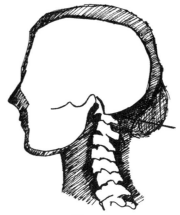

Fig. 8
Occipital Joint

Positive Thinking!

Our thoughts have an enormous effect on our bodies. A frightened person automatically draws his shoulders up to his ears (a protective instinct) just as a person suffering from psychological stress walks sluggishly with slumped shoulders.

One of the questions that kinesiologists ask is, "What are the psychological effects of human activity on human behavior?" They work with the body to find out what is wrong or where blockages are by "asking" the body where the problem lies (*for more details see the section on Applied Kinesiology on page 56*). Our imagination (psyche) plays a major role in

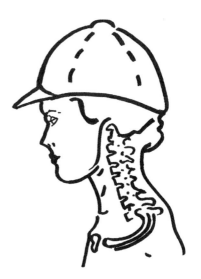

Fig. 9
Exercise to free occipital joint. Rider gazes at the ground by looking between the horse's ears.

our performance. For example, if riders think about earlier mistakes during jumping or dressage performances, they will automatically make the same incorrect motions again and again, leading to intense frustration. Any mistake made during a performance must be let go of as soon as it happens so as to allow the mind and body the best chance of making a change during the next moments of the performance. Sometimes people think that they must replay mistakes in order to avoid making them again, but the opposite is actually true. When a mistake is made, it is very important to think instead about the right way to perform the movement and not to dwell on the mistake. Whatever pictures are replayed in the mind the most will influence the motion of the body. Positive thinking energizes the rider because it frees the mind from negative thoughts and prevents the release of stress hormones. If athletes concentrate on negative thoughts, their bodies could react so extremely that they will be unable to finish their performance. Positive thinking is especially important in horseback riding because it is one of the most complicated of all sports, and involves the "thinking" of not just one, but two beings!

GRIMACING IS GLOOMY

A positive attitude creates positive communications. This is essential for several reasons. First, it helps the rider focus on a positive outcome. Second, a positive attitude creates freedom in the movement of energy, while negative attitudes drain and block energy. Third, the body acts out the thoughts, and thus the attitude (positive or negative) will flow from the rider to the horse.

Some riders grimace when they ride. This may develop because of fear, anxiety, determination, concentration, or many other psychological factors, but at some point it becomes a habit. The rider's jaws are clamped together and sometimes they grind their teeth. This tension in their jaw transfers to their head, then to their neck and chest, and all the way down to their pelvis, automatically blocking the pelvis from following the horse's movement.

Riders cannot be supple when they have a grimace on their face. To become aware of this effect try clamping your jaws and shaking your head from side to side. Then open your mouth a little bit and shake your head from side to side. You will instantly feel the different between the two situations; it is much easier to move even your head when your jaw is relaxed.

Letting Go

Riders can cause tension in their bodies and have trouble communicating with their horse if they think too hard while riding. In this situation the left side of the brain (the logical part) works too hard. The left brain cannot handle things simultaneously; it only handles thoughts and actions one at a time. Riding requires performing many actions at the same time, so left brain riders will not be able to respond quickly enough to the situation to make the performance flow smoothly and correctly. The rider needs to use their left brain before a performance to imagine the perfect ride and how it will feel. Then, during the actual performance, they must be aware of "letting go" and allowing the right side of the brain to take over the coordination of all of the necessary actions. The left brain should only observe the performance and must not be allowed to interrupt while the right brain allows the pre-planned motions to occur, almost subconsciously. Once the performance is over, the left brain can be called upon to comment on the performance and to think about how the rider wants it to happen the next time. During a lesson or practice ride this switch between left and right sides of the brain can happen many times, and is a very effective way to use the brain's psychology for learning.

Fear

Unfortunately many riding instructors and riders know too little about the meaning fear has for learning motion. Not only do cognitive processes play a role in riders' performances, but emotions also play a significant role. Emotional attitudes such as an attraction or aversion to a certain situation will affect learning and performing motions. Each of us would like to fulfill the challenges offered by horseback riding, but we are sometimes held back by fear and anxiety, which come to the surface when we are faced with a discouraging situation.

Fear is simply an emotional state. A person in this state expects a threat. Fear evokes a lack of enthusiasm, reluctance, or uneasiness. When riding instructors yell at their students or impatiently wait for the student to follow their commands, they generate fear in their students. Such instructors are emotionally abusing their students. Fear can also result if someone must deal with a situation where he knows for a fact that he will fail. If this occurs in any teaching situation, the instructor is over-estimating the student's capabilities, which will lead to a lack of trust between instructor and student, as well as to some potentially unsafe situations.

Fear is also caused when a rider knows that his own abilities are not good enough to fulfill the demands made by the instructor. The relationship between instructor and student is a power relationship; whether the instructor realizes it or not, they hold a lot of power. Students want to impress their instructors; they want to be liked by the instructor. If the instructor makes a demand on the student based on their own ability level or perspective rather than that of the student, fear may result. Instructors need to tailor their expectations to the emotional and physical abilities of each rider. Riders need to recognize when fear of their instructor may be getting in the way of their learning, and either discuss this with the instructor, or find a different instructor who does not inspire such fear. Learning will be impossible with too much of this kind of fear.

In assessing a particular lesson or task, the current situation may not play a very important role in students' fear levels. Past experiences do play a major role, however, in how a rider reacts to a particular situation. Past experiences of failure or unsuccessful attempts have a prolonged negative effect on a rider's judgment. If a rider has had a bad experience in the past, he or she will have trouble assessing the current situation objectively.

A democratic approach to teaching horseback riding reduces the fear factor because the decision to act in a particular situation is left up to the rider. An authoritative style of teaching forces the student to deal with a specific exercise, whether or not she wants to. This sparks fear in students and can lead both to failures and to dangerous situations for rider and horse.

TYPES OF FEAR

The following categories of the general term "fear" should be considered for teaching and riding purposes. Although they are closely related we have separated them for clarification purposes.
- General anxiety
- Fear caused by orientation problems
- Fear of the unknown
- Fear of actual things
- Fear of anticipation

General Anxiety

Fear occurs when certain situations, objects or thoughts (temporary or over a certain period of time) cause inner uneasiness. Anxiety, on the other hand, is a *chronic* state of mind, which always reveals itself in performance situations. Sources of anxiety are numerous: it can be caused by a genetic disorder, a person's early life experiences, or a difficulty with career demands. Children cannot develop healthy self-esteem if parents constantly criticize them. This constant criticism can lay a foundation for disappointments and failure later on in life. Children in this kind of environment can develop serious feelings of worthlessness over a period of years. They feel that they cannot do anything right and may have problems establishing a stable personality.

A person's anxiety level is closely related to how afraid they are of failure, punishment and performance. This condition can also arise later on in life. The level of fear a person suffers in a particular situation depends on the level of general anxiety in their life; in other words, to deal with fear, one must first deal with anxiety.

Fear Caused by Orientation Problems

Loss of orientation refers to uncertainty about one's surroundings and triggers fear in both rider and horse. This, naturally, leads to problems in the learning process. Darkness, strange surroundings or unusual ground conditions, for example, limit a rider and horse's ability to get oriented. In these cases, fear is a *perception problem* and produces internal uncertainty, which, in turn, leads to problems in performance. Typical causes of such orientation problems in horseback riding include anticipated (i.e. show grounds) or unanticipated (i.e. being lost or encountering something new in a familiar space) foreign environments, new types of jumps that seem to be impassable, treacherous forest paths, etc.

Fear of the Unknown
Fear of the unknown is caused when a rider cannot anticipate the outcome of **new situations** or **new demands.** This is why many students tend to avoid new situations or challenges. This form of fear is a kind of security measure that shields the rider from extremely demanding situations. In dealing with this kind of fear riders can slowly feel their way though a new action or motion or situation, perhaps with the help of an instructor. Taking one's time and not pushing ahead too quickly gives the emotional center in the brain time to adapt and relax and may avoid the fear response that blocks learning and performance. With practice the mindset of desiring to avoid new things begins to disappear.

Fear of Actual Things
This type of fear is defined as the fear of **certain objects, persons** or **situations**. For example, a rider is afraid of jumping over certain obstacles because he is afraid that his horse could refuse the jump or fall. In another case, a rider is afraid of the instructor because in a previous instance he or she used authoritative and insulting instructional methods and hurt the student's self-confidence.

Fear of Anticipation
Fear of anticipation simply means the **fear of fear** itself. Expressions such as, "I don't **ever** want that to happen again!" or "If I just **think** about it I get scared!" illustrate this type of fear. Fear of anticipation is deeply ingrained in a person's mind and is part of their character. They do not have to actually experience a situation to be afraid; just imagining this fearful object or situation can make them literally afraid.

SOURCES OF FEAR
Each person who learns to ride brings his own "baggage" with him; a set of personal experiences that has an effect on how he will handle

new situations that he is faced with. These experiences stem from the diverse set of situations that each person has been through during his lifetime. However, since riding instructors cannot be aware of all of these past experiences, they must have exceptional instructional skills to be able to recognize and appropriately handle all kinds of responses that they may observe in their students throughout the process of learning to ride. Students must be able to recognize their instructors as people who are open and willing to deal with difficulties and to discuss any problems or discomfort their students might have.

The way in which a child is raised plays an important role in how that child will handle fear as an adult. During childhood and young adulthood, children develop values that will stay with them throughout their lives. They also learn at an early age to either adapt to society's norms or to rebel against them. The way a child learns and develops these values and norms determines, to a great extent, how he or she will behave as an adult.

Parents who raise their children under extreme pressure to succeed usually employ harsh punishments, forbid certain experiences without reason, and use commands and orders to spur their children on. This can lead to the child's having difficulty accepting and learning from constructive criticism, which cripples the child's personality development. This method of child rearing results in an increased tendency towards general anxiety in children and in later adulthood.

Furthermore, if a person expects pain or bodily harm in a certain situation, he will be afraid. A person who has suffered an injury during jumping or who has witnessed a friend's fall or heard about a serious accident may develop a fear of jumping. People may also take their negative experiences and apply them, without real reason, to a new situation. This is a very difficult situation to deal with for instructors. They may have difficulty determining where the fear came from and how to avoid the situations that trigger the fear.

Failure, too, can lead to fear. If a student has experienced failure in one sport, the resulting blow to the student's self-esteem is often transferred to each new sport. This can mean that a riding student with a painful experience in the 100-meter hurdles, for example, may have trouble relaxing and letting go of his anxiety when jumping with a horse.

Fear of failure can result when one's expectations do not coincide with the actual performance level or ability. Positive performance experiences raise a student's expectations of himself and improve his motivation, while negative performance experiences lower his expectations and motivation. Yet it is also important that students learn how to handle perceived failure. If students never experience failure, they may develop a fear of it anyway (fear of the unknown), whereas if the instructor can help students understand "failures" as wonderful learning opportunities, some of the fear of failure may disappear. A simple example of this is falling off the horse. A student who has never fallen off a horse may develop a fear of falling off, either because of fear that it will hurt or fear that falling off will make her a "bad rider." If an instructor can incorporate lessons in how to fall off as well as discussing why a rider might fall off and what she can learn from that experience, some of the fear of this "failure" may dissipate. Without the fear, the actual event is less likely to occur, but if it does happen, the student will be more likely to be able to integrate it into her learning program rather than allowing it to throw her off track.

There is another aspect to fear of failure that riders often deal with, especially when riding in groups or when riding in competition. Normally, a typical athlete strives to improve her level of performance and, at the same time, has very high expectations of herself. This, combined with the presence of constant competition and performance pressure in student riding groups can cause the anxiety of fear of failure to occur.

Additionally students riding in groups may experience fear of embarrassment. They may be afraid that they will be laughed at or unfavorably compared with their riding companions. The instructor can set the tone by emphasizing that learning to ride is not about showing off with the horse or looking down at weaker riders but is rather about each horse and rider combination learning and developing through their own experiences, both individually and in a group.

SIGNS OF FEAR AND INFLUENCES ON BEHAVIOR

Visual signs of fear include an increase in pulse, very tense or cramped muscles, increase in blood pressure, enlargement of the pupils, shaking, sweating, redness or paleness of the face or lack of appetite. Certain other emotions often signal fear such as doubt, insecurity, and hesitation. These may result in passivity, extreme activity, or aggressive behavior.

Fearful riders tend to exaggerate the demands that the instructor is making or the difficulty of the task. These exaggerations cause a student to misjudge a situation and can result in mistakes or even accidents. In a jumping course, for example, a fearful rider does not have as much influence on his horse and may change speed either too early or too late for the horse to jump. A person's sensory organs (ears, skin, eyes, balancing mechanisms, and muscle senses) are constrained in situations controlled by fear.

Furthermore, students are not able to fully comprehend an instructor's verbal commands or advice when controlled by fear. Their visual judgment is also impaired. Their muscle sensors cannot react quickly enough or precisely enough because fear impairs their central nervous system by blocking the signals from the brain to the muscles.

Serious mistakes can result from the lack of muscle function. A rider who is scared can become "paralyzed" thus leaving the horse to his own devices to figure out what to do. A horse in this situation can become confused by the erratic motions of his rider, will not understand what he is supposed to do, and may react in ways very different from how the rider wants him to react. The rider's aids are not consistent, which causes the horse to react in the wrong way.

FEAR IS NOT ALL BAD!

A low level of fear or stress can actually help a rider's (and a horse's) performance to be top quality. This is because adrenaline causes a higher degree of awareness, which can lead to a positive "sharpness" in the performance. This can be seen in horses who like to "show off" when they are braided up and riding in a competition. However, if the fear reaches a certain level, unique to each individual, it will seriously inhibit performance.

Aggression/Frustration
Aggression in Horseback Riding
Aggressive behavior is not an uncommon occurrence in our society today, nor is it uncommon in horseback riding. In this section I will try to get behind this aggressiveness and discuss the roots and causes for such behavior. To illustrate how aggressive behavior can be triggered I will use two typical examples.

THE TERM "AGGRESSION"
The term "aggression" comes from the Latin word for "attack" and refers to purposely harmful behavior. If you step on someone's foot on purpose you are showing aggressive behavior. If this happens by accident, then it is altogether different. It may still be perceived as aggressive, but your intension was not aggressive.

Aggression also often includes assumptions of bodily harm. However, harm can also be done with words, and this may be termed emotional aggression. People who engage in this kind of aggression harm the soul and spirit of others and also cause psychological injury.

The term "aggressive" can refer to a behavior or to a person. An aggressive behavior may be performed by anyone, and may not be in character for an individual. If somebody has a bad day and is grumpy and upset, they may engage in aggressive behaviors every now and then, but these are usually temporary and the person may feel remorse afterwards and seek to apologize for the behavior. An "aggressive person" tends to refer to a person with a more lasting personality characteristic, which may have been caused by a frustrating experience that permanently damaged the person's personality. These people will tend to infuse everything they do with aggression, and may not feel remorse or seek to apologize or make changes in their behavior.

THEORIES AND HYPOTHESES REGARDING AGGRESSION
– The Frustration/Aggression Hypothesis
We will now examine some case studies in order to explore a few common theories and hypotheses regarding aggression, as well as to gain some insight into how aggressive behavior can be handled.

Frustration is a forced rejection of the fulfillment of self-determined goals, wishes and needs. A hypothesis is an assumption or an unproved statement. This hypothesis suggests that aggression is always rooted in a frustration. Using this hypothesis one can say that the occurrence of aggressive behavior is always based on the presence of frustration; while the opposite is not true since the existence of frustration does not always lead to aggressive behavior.

Aggression in Action—Situation A: A twenty-something-year-old riding student is taking riding lessons with two friends. On this particular day the riding instructor is not pleased with the student's seat and her influence on the horse. Corrections keep flying at her constantly. The student really wants to apply her instructor's commands, but the horse is not responding to her aids. Each time the student tries to complete the task her instructor gives her, she fails. Her instructor becomes more and more unsatisfied until he finally tells the student that it might be a good idea to just quit completely. After this terse comment the student becomes even more determined, presses her lips together and uses the time when the instructor is not watching to kick her horse (not very gently). After the hour is over, the student leads her horse through the stable hallway. On the way, the horse stops and turns to another horse in the stable. The student yanks vigorously on the reins several times to get the horse to continue walking. She then ties him up to remove the saddle. When she is about to lead him into the wash stall she sees that it is already being used. She yells at the person in the wash area, "Hey! Can't you see that I'm waiting?! Hurry up!"

Interpretation of Situation A according to the Frustration/Aggression Hypothesis: Situation A shows a rider who fails to complete a certain task during a lesson. Every rider wants her horse to accept her aids and to react appropriately. This makes riding an enjoyable experience. This rider, however, cannot find that comfortable feel, at least for the moment.

She is frustrated with the riding situation because the lesson is not leading anywhere. The instructor is trying to help the student by giving all the commands he knows to correct her actions, but this constant negative input distracts the rider even more, making it impossible for her to concentrate on herself, let alone her horse. Less *would* be more in this situation, if we look at it from a teaching perspective.

Not only does the rider realize that she is not being successful, but she also has the instructor informing her of every little slip-up along the way. At this point she is already approaching her limit. The student experiences the pain of failure, resulting in increasing tension in her body, and although she would like to be given some slack from the instructor, she lets herself be controlled by the instructor's authority and supremacy and thus becomes even more frustrated and tense inside.

The first one to feel the effects of this situation is the horse, who receives harmful kicks in the sides from our frustrated student. The poor horse cannot defend himself! About to explode and full of tension and frustration, the student exits the riding arena and takes her immense frustration out on her horse at the very next opportunity. The poor fellow rider in the wash stall gets a few verbal lashings himself, even though he has nothing to do with the inner frustrations of the student.

Where Does Aggression Come From Under the Frustration/Aggression Hypothesis?

Through lifelong observation I have come to realize that common aggressive behaviors can always be traced back to frustrations. Of course, outside observers cannot always recognize such aggressive behavior as being caused by disappointment, deprivation, or rejection in certain people. Outsiders (such as the instructor in Situation A) appear to be content with NOT knowing! However, they cannot and should not be content with ignoring the situation because it will only escalate further and further within the student. People may learn to repress openly aggressive behavior since it is not socially accepted, and they can learn to hide their true feelings and frustrations from whomever they choose. The problem is that this does not deal with the root problem. The frustrations and aggressive feelings become repressed, which is not healthy.

Repressed feelings are simply postponed, distorted, and pushed away for the time being. They can emerge at other times in other situations where aggressive behavior would have little or no consequence for the aggressor. If the student in our example had shown any aggressive behavior during the lesson it would have led to punishment or a scolding. Since the student could not let her frustration out on the instructor, she let it out on her helpless and defenseless horse and the person in the wash stall, fully knowing that her behavior would not have any significant consequences.

Instead of leading to distortions or denials, frustrations can, under certain circumstances, also lead to regression (a deterioration of personality), depending on the character of the person and her personal attitudes. In other words, too many disappointments, failures, or "neediness" can cause a person to lose her self-esteem and develop unreceptive, passive behavior. Such people pull back into their shells and grieve (or feel sorry for themselves). In essence, they turn their aggression against themselves, and beat themselves up inside for everything that goes wrong. This is also not a healthy situation and can require counseling.

Prevention of Aggression Based on the Frustration/Aggression Hypothesis

The frustration and aggression seen in Situation A could have been avoided if the student had experienced a different method of teaching. Her instructor was using a purely command-oriented teaching method, which cannot adjust to the needs, problems, or wishes of each student. The instructor simply dictates actions to the student, employing strictly riding techniques instead of dealing with the student's and horse's current individual challenges. If the instructor had chosen instead to try to understand the student and empathize with her, without placing more pressure on her to perform, they may have been able to work together to find a solution to the struggle that the student was encountering. Teaching in this way would have won the confidence of the student, who would have felt understood and not so inadequate. The instructor also would have learned a lot about his student's feelings, thoughts, opinions, and attitudes, which could have allowed the misunderstandings, disappointments and frustrations to be avoided, and thus probably the aggression as well.

In a group setting instructors must be careful to balance their comments towards all of the students so that one student does not feel picked on. If a student does feel criticized over and over again, he or she can develop inner psychological anxiety, which cannot be easily repaired. This can show itself as frustration and aggression and may be taken out on their horse and fellow students, or may be inwardly directed towards themselves.

Students may also develop inner anxiety and frustration with themselves because they feel that they have failed to meet their own goals; thus the pressure comes from within rather than from the instructor.

The instructor's role in this situation is to recognize what is going on inside the student and take the initiative to discuss the situation with the student and develop a plan to help the student both to deal with the disappointment of not meeting her goals and to help her plan a path that will lead her closer to her goals.

This example illustrates the necessity for a democratic style of teaching using experience oriented methods *(see Instructor Section, page 159)* to make it possible for the interests and needs of all involved to be taken into consideration and met.

THEORIES AND HYPOTHESES REGARDING AGGRESSION
– The Aggression as Learned Behavior Hypothesis

This theory supports the assumption that aggressive social interaction is primarily learned in two ways:
- By seeing or hearing aggressive behavior in others (learning by example / learning through observation)
- By experiencing that aggression is often successful in getting one's own way and that it also works as a defense (learning by success / learning by reinforcement)

Aggression in Action—Situation B: A 50-year-old stockbroker likes to ride after work at a barn for recreational riders. The instructor's way of teaching the group is to give each one an individual task. The stockbroker—the only one in the group who really sticks out—has a very determined and resolute way of riding. His facial expressions and his body language (lips pressed together, fierce eyes, and abrupt movements) reveal his inner tension. He also shows very little feel or harmony with the horse. One day the instructor sees this and urges the rider (again) to deal with the horse in a more relaxed way. It should not be about going to the Olympics, she says, but about relaxing and enjoying horseback riding. Nevertheless, his behavior keeps getting worse and worse until he finally jerks the reins very forcefully, digs his heels into the horse's sides and yells, "Alright, that's enough! I've had it! I'm the master here, you dumb animal!"

Interpretation of Situation B according to the Aggression as Learned Behavior Hypothesis: In this situation the 50-year-old stockbroker rides very ambitiously and demands more of himself and his horse than either are able to give. He is a successful businessman who does not want to show any signs of weakness, either at work or on a horse. He projects his stressful work onto his recreational activities because he cannot let go of the high performance norms he has internalized during his career. Instead of giving *himself* the blame for the bad situation, he makes it very clear, through his entire behavior (verbally, physically, and facially), that he assigns all blame to the horse. He does not separate recreation from career and cannot relax and forget the daily pressures he deals with at work. The "dog-eat-dog" methods of survival in the business world are projected onto horseback riding.

Where Does Aggression Come From Under the Aggression as Learned Behavior Hypothesis?

In order to find the reasons for such behavior, we do not have to look farther than our own daily lives. We see it around us, and experience it in many ways each day. A supervisor may use an aggressive tone of voice with an employee. Why does he do this? The employee is unable to defend himself against his boss' verbal abuse (without risking losing his job). The supervisor is behaving as many other supervisors do and presumably in the same way that his supervisors behave, using this aggressive pattern. If a person of higher rank or power shows aggressive behaviors to a person of lower rank, it is natural for the subordinate to copy this aggressive behavior. The subordinate sees that his supervisor has become successful by behaving in this way, so may assume that this behavior is expected in successful people. This illustrates the learning by example part of the theory.

Studies have also been done about how humans imitate and reproduce observed aggressive behavior; for example, behaviors seen while watching a movie. There is a lot of aggression and violence shown on television, in computer games, and in the theaters, so some aggressive behaviors may be a result of this overexposure to these types of behavior, or learning by observation.

Another theory of how aggressive behavior is learned is learning by reinforcement, or learning by success. This theory cannot explain exactly why a person begins to act aggressively, but offers a possible explanation of why a person might continue to use this behavior. A common use of aggressive behavior is for purposes of achieving personal success, for example by exerting pressure in favor of one's own goals and personal interests. A person may act aggressively towards another if the other person does nothing to defend himself. By asserting himself in this situation, the aggressor takes a step toward fulfilling his own wishes. When this succeeds, he has experienced positive reinforcement for his behavior and will tend to repeat this behavior in future situations.

A classic example of learning by reinforcement is a child who yells and screams to convince his parents to give him what he wants. If the parents give in, the child learns that yelling and screaming is a successful behavior, and will tend to repeat it. The same thing happens in adulthood, although it may be more subtle, and therefore difficult to recognize.

Prevention of Aggression Based on the Aggression as Learned Behavior Hypothesis

Imitation of aggressive behavior occurs in horseback riding as well as in our daily lives. Riding instructors have a reputation for yelling and displaying aggressive behavior towards their students as well as the horses. Younger riders identify these instructors as role models and thus want to become "just like" them, which can include the aggressive behavior. Riders want to achieve success and see the success of their instructors. Aggressive behavior is something that is easy to copy; easier than copying their instructor's finely tuned sense of feel or knowledge about riding and training. In general, people's behavior is strongly dependent on what examples they are given in life.

Aggression may also be learned through interactions between members of a riding class or people who board their horses at the same barn. There may be pressure on the instructor or barn owner to admire and esteem riders with successful careers and high positions. These successful businessmen and businesswomen may display aggressive and strongly controlling behaviors learned at work, and instructors must be careful to balance their attention so that other members of the group do not pick up these aggressive behaviors simply because these members of the group may appear to be more successful than they are. It is important for instructors to be sure that riding students do not get their way through use of aggressive behavior, or this behavior may spread to all members of the riding group, having a drastic effect. If harmful words have succeeded in silencing someone, aggressive individuals can easily take the lead and put themselves in the center. They can then decide the fates of others and tell the whole group what to do and how to treat people. In these situations instructors must see through such behavior and try to give the group a common goal and stress common interests.

Use of the dialogue concept of teaching and learning can help prevent this type of aggression. First, it levels the playing field, so that riders may not feel so inadequate when standing next to their instructors, even if the instructor does have more skills. Second, it allows a lot more interaction between instructor and student, and a discussion of how different techniques are required for success in the business world and on a horse may ensue. Also an instructor who is committed to the dialogue concept is unlikely to display aggressive language and behavior when interacting with horses and students, so may model a more healthy way of interacting.

The Seat

Each rider is a unique human being with a unique body. History, culture, and life circumstances have increased the imbalances in our physical bodies and have disrupted the balance between mind and body. Most riders believe in the importance of having a "correct seat" but are hard pressed to define what that means. Too often a "correct seat" is defined by specific forms, and riding instructors see their job as molding riders to fit those forms. In reality, a "correct seat" is unique to the individual, taking into consideration the variations of each person's body. Once a few basic alignments are in place, it is the functioning of the muscles that allows the body to have the movement necessary to flow with and correctly influence the horse. The seat is multidimensional, including the body, mind, motion and laws of physics. The rider's seat is where the dialogue between the horse's back and the rider's pelvis takes place. An effective seat is upright: interactive, elastic, balanced, solid and soft. Corrections and changes most often begin with the hips or the head in order to achieve the correct seat.

It is important to remember that the seat includes the 'whole' person. The seat is divided into the following areas:

- Overall
- Head
- Neck & Shoulders
- Torso
- Pelvis
- Legs

This section will walk through the rider's body, noting characteristics of what would be considered correct in each area, as well as common *deviations* that individuals often use as they figure out the best way to use that part of the body. These are often referred to as problems or mistakes, but using negative terms is not effective in helping riders come closer to their individual ideal. Calling something a *mistake* is only correct when the horse and rider do not make any steps towards achieving the original intention, such as a rider who asks the horse for a canter, but gets no response from the horse. If the rider is in the trot and asks for the canter, but succeeds only in getting a faster trot, this is not a mistake; it is a *deficiency*. *Deficiencies* are when some parts of the intention are realized, but some parts still need to be improved or realized. *Deviations* are students' attempts to realize their original intention, and may not be correct or be the best way to solve the task given them, but they are not mistakes. Often times the root of those deviations is found elsewhere in the body, so the instructor must be aware of the ways that the rider's body and mind are connected in order to help the rider discover the more effective and efficient solution. For example, a rider who is getting red in the face is not making a mistake, but is probably either holding his breath or becoming frustrated with himself or his horse, two common deviations from the ideal, relaxed, breathing frame of mind and body that is the overall intention or goal. Another example is a rider who is sitting in the chair seat. This is not a mistake, but is a deviation from the ideal, balanced position, perhaps resulting from the rider's attempts to feel secure and in control of the horse.

As well as describing common deviations riders may feel and instructors may notice, some possible solutions may be suggested. The most important point to remember for effectiveness in achieving the ideal for each horse and rider is flexibility and creativity in deciding how to approach a particular deviation that a rider is experiencing.

> *The most important point to remember for effectiveness in achieving the ideal for each horse and rider is flexibility and creativity in deciding how to approach a particular deviation that a rider is experiencing.*

The Correct Overall Seat

There is no question that a rider must always sit upright in order to use his center of gravity effectively in dialogue with the horse. The problem is, however, that most people are unable to sit upright and stay relaxed at the same time because their muscles are not trained enough.

The rider's seat is the communicator between the horse's back and the rider's pelvis. Corrections and changes must begin with the hips in order to achieve the correct seat. Brugger's example of the cogwheel (Fig. 10) shows clearly how changes made in the hip region affect the rest of the body.

Each rider needs to strive for an "interactive seat," which is elastic, balanced, and upright. Two lines to look for are: shoulder-hip-heel and elbow-forearm-reins-horse's mouth. The body is a unit, and each part affects every other part. Our minds and bodies, as well as our muscles, must work together in partnership.

ALIGNMENT (ELASTIC, BALANCED & UPRIGHT)

A straight line from a rider's head down to his or her seat defines a vertical seat. This line must be perpendicular with the ground. Each joint of the spine, which connects

Fig. 10
Brugger's Cogwheel Model

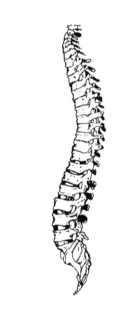

Fig. 11
Correctly Aligned Spine

RIDER — Effective Teaching & Riding   97

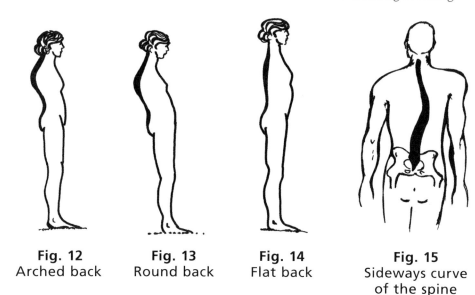

| Fig. 12 | Fig. 13 | Fig. 14 | Fig. 15 |
Arched back | Round back | Flat back | Sideways curve of the spine

the head, arms, and pelvis, must be upright and yet flexible. Each of the vertebra offers some movement that allows the appearance of no movement overall. A flat "S" shape of the spine (Fig. 11) supports upright posture, which is long and tall without being held tense. The actual form of the spine is impossible to see without an x-ray, but only a correctly aligned spine can provide the correct elasticity needed to maintain the ideal posture and to use the driving aids effectively.

Any other position of the spine, such as an arched back (Fig. 12), round back (Fig. 13), flat back (Fig. 14) or a sideways curve in the spine (Fig. 15) brings the rider away from the ideal vertical position.

A DEEP SEAT

A deep seat is one where the rider's weight is sinking evenly down both sides of the body towards the ground and the rider appears to be one with the horse, sitting "in" the horse rather than "on" the horse. In the deep seat, the weight of the rider's body begins at the head, goes down through the center, splits equally at the rider's crotch and goes down the inside of the legs and out toward the ground through the heel. The deep seat is essential in allowing the horse to comfortably carry the rider in balance, and for the rider to move with the horse in a following motion.

A person's body structure is very important for their motion, and because each person has an individual body structure, instructors must carefully study each individual when trying to solve their specific problems.

Wide-set hips are helpful for developing a deep seat. If a person has narrow-set hips, he or she will sit more "on top of" the horse than "in" the horse. People with narrow-set hips tend to use the reins more to counterbalance this. Unfortunately, even stretching and lengthening the inside thigh muscles will not make their seat any deeper because of the position of the bones of the hips and pelvis. A rider with this body type needs to find a horse that is of a suitable size (i.e. not too large or wide) so that it matches their hip width. If a person has a horse with too narrow of a back their knees will be too close together, and they will not be able to use their legs to drive effectively. Smooth swinging on a horse with a very narrow back can also prove to be very difficult. A horse with a back that is too wide can also be a problem. In this situation a person's legs are so extremely spread apart that their pelvis becomes blocked and they are "helpless" as far as being able to use their aids effectively on the horse.

COMPARISON BETWEEN A RIDER AND A SHIP'S MAST
If commands like "Head up! Knees down! Hands higher! Close your legs!" etc. actually worked, we could say that the human body is just a wooden puppet on strings. Instructors who use these kinds of commands undoubtedly mean well. They want their students to sit correctly so that they can effectively drive the horse.

The Human "Mast"
To make myself clear, I do not mean a solid, wooden mast, but rather a flexible one, like the human spine, with different elements connected together (in the human it is the vertebrae that are connected). These elements form sections that are stacked above each other: the head, cervical (neck) vertebrae, thoracic (middle back) vertebrae and the lumbar (lower back) vertebrae. The ribs keep the chest section (thoracic vertebrae) stable and fairly nonflexible. Movement in this region is further stabilized because the disks between the

vertebrae are thinner than those in the lumbar region. In the lumbar section of the spine there are no ribs to stabilize movement so the vertebrae are dependent on the person's muscles in that area for stability. If all the muscles in the lumbar region are well developed people have good range of motion in this area as well as stability. If they are underdeveloped, however, people experience lower back pain. Lower down we have the tailbone (*sacrum*). This is made up of 5 vertebrae that have been "fused" together and thus are very stable and anchored with ligaments to the pelvis.

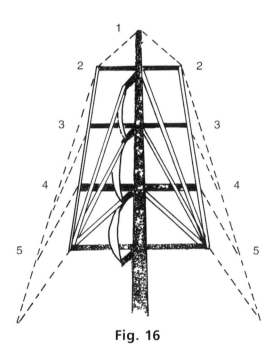

Fig. 16

The human body is essentially built like a ship's mast. Figure 16 illustrates the similar structures between a ship's mast and the human spine. This comparison demonstrates how any tiny motion has an immediate and direct effect on the rest of the system. Changes in the shoulders (2) automatically cause changes to occur in the entire muscle system, for example in the chest area (3), also in the hips (4), in the knees (5) and even in the feet.

COMMON DEVIATIONS OF THE OVERALL SEAT

An upright walking posture begins (literally) with the feet. The same is true for a good riding posture. The smallest change in the feet has an effect on the body that extends from the feet to the head and back. Problems with the head and shoulders can often be traced back to a rigid heel. In other words, riders who have heels that are either too high or too low, or who turn their feet inwards can consequently have trouble with their head and neck. Additionally, feet that are turned inwards turn the stirrups away from the horse's side, which then prevents the rider from being able to swing properly with the horse.

In order to use aids most effectively riders must be able to extend their spines. However, extension is often over-used and exaggerated, especially in dressage. Dressage riders tend to have their stirrups too long and because they overextend their bodies, they tend to put more pressure into the stirrups than necessary. This blocks the pelvis and prevents flowing motion with the horse. The horse feels the extended position as more pressure and will become tense and agitated.

Although judges and instructors may think that this extended sitting posture looks correct, it is not effective. The length of the stirrups must be set for each individual. Riders need to experiment with different stirrup lengths to find the one that enables their pelvis to swing as smoothly as possible with the horse. Through the process of elimination riders can feel when the stirrup length allows for optimal flexibility and suppleness. As a rule of thumb, the ball of the foot should be in contact with the stirrup, with the hips relaxed so that the ankle can move freely. If the toes are in contact with the stirrup, the heel drops and the ankles become locked producing stiffness through the whole body. The same thing happens if the feet slide too far into the stirrups, causing the toe to point to the ground and the heel to be higher than the stirrups.

Despite instructors' efforts, it is not always the case that students find the correct seat. Even though instructors may use good descriptions and eloquent commands, their students cannot necessarily sit well. This is caused by numerous and various challenges, which make it difficult, and at times impossible, for students to put this good advice to use. Instructors must be aware of the fact that the origins of visible problems are not always in obvious places. Neck pain may be caused, for example, by an incorrect heel position. If instructors only correct problems where they see them, riders will have difficulty making long-term corrections. Instructors must discover the root of the problem in order to figure out a solution.

The Correct Position of the Head

What goes on both inside and outside of the head is extremely important for effective riding. Perhaps what is in the head is more important than its position on the body! What observers see in the eyes and facial expression of the rider reveals what is going on inside and will lead to appropriate suggestions. The rider should have soft eyes that focus with intent, but not too much concentration, on the task at hand. While it is often difficult to smile and ride, having a mouth that is free of tightness allows the rider the most freedom to respond to the horse and to the instructor. The head should sit squarely on the neck with flexibility to turn as needed. The rider's "inner eye" should feel the weight of the head traveling down through the center of the body, gaining weight from the body as it goes downward. When this weight reaches the rider's crotch, it splits and continues downward and out the heels. While the body weight is traveling downward due to gravity's force, the rider appears to be carrying his upper body flexibly upright like a puppet with strings in the clouds.

COMMON DEVIATIONS IN HEAD POSITION AND USE
The Human Head: A Weighty Matter
The human body is an amazing organism, but it has one imperfection: the head. An adult human head weighs a remarkable 11 pounds and is much too heavy for the delicate neck vertebrae on which it rests. These delicate neck vertebrae are unable to hold the head completely vertical to the rest of the body. Furthermore, the muscles in the neck are not strong enough to keep the head straight and relaxed without becoming tight at the same time.

Because today's jobs and careers continually require less and less physical activity from us, our muscles grow weaker and weaker. Our daily movements require the use of only certain muscles, which, of course, causes some muscles to be over-developed and some to be under-developed. These muscular imbalances harm riders more than any other athletes.

Horses must be able to maintain their balance with a rider sitting on their backs. However, riders with muscular imbalances will have great difficulty helping a horse maintain its balance. These riders will be unable to coordinate their motions with those of the horse. In other words, their muscles will be unable to "tune into" the horse's rhythm, and they will be unable to have an effective dialogue with the horse. A rider with an unbalanced head will find it impossible to balance other areas of his body as well as balancing his horse.

The Head Initiates Motion

The importance of the head in motion and posture is unfortunately underestimated. If the head is not held correctly riders cannot allow their bodies to relax. The occipital joint (Fig. 17) and the connection in the spine between the 7th neck vertebra and the first chest vertebra (Fig. 18) are very important.

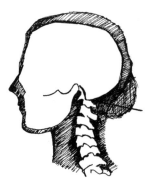

**Fig. 17
Occipital Joint**

The occipital joint is where the skull and the first neck vertebra meet. It is also known as the atlas joint. To find the occipital joint, use two fingers to feel for a small "knot" just below the base of the skull. It is very important for this joint to be loose and relaxed because it determines how smoothly a rider's body is able to move with the horse's rhythm. This joint is often blocked, however, due to incorrect posture of the head (tilted to one side or another, forward or backward). If riders have bad posture the occipital neck muscles will tend to shorten over time.

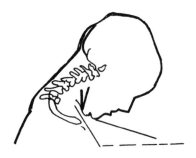

**Fig. 18
The connection in the spine between the 7th neck vertebra and the first chest vertebra**

— EXERCISES FOR THE HEAD —

Puppet

To "free" the occipital joint you must imagine your head being "pulled" upwards, as if the top of your head were attached to a string. Instead of trying to look straight ahead, riders should allow their chin to tilt slightly downward, which allows them to comfortably gaze ahead and automatically frees the occipital joint.

Fig. 19

Neck Massage and Stretch

Self-massages can also help free the occipital joint. Place the first, middle, and ring fingers of both hands between the base of the skull and the first neck vertebra.

Gently massage these muscles. After massaging the muscles riders should then stretch these muscles to retain the suppleness gained from the massage.

Fig. 20

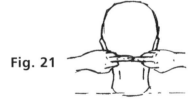

With one hand place the tip of the middle finger on the occipital joint and the tip of the middle finger of the other hand on top. Pull your elbows outward.

Fig. 21

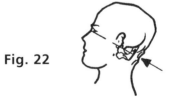

This puts pressure on the joint.

Fig. 22

As you maintain your hand position, stretch your head back and then your chin forward. Hold each position for 10 seconds and repeat from the beginning 3 times.

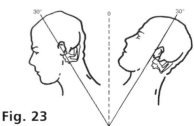

Fig. 23

> **The Owl**
>
> **Starting Point:** Look straight ahead.
>
> **Movement:** Turn your head from side to side on the centerline axis, while holding your chin on a steady level. Take hold of your left shoulder with your right hand (not too tightly) and turn your head slowly over one shoulder and then over the other. After a few repetitions let go of your shoulders, let your head sink slowly onto your sternum and inhale deeply. This lets the muscles release and relax. Then do the same exercise with the other hand holding onto the other shoulder.
>
> **Results:**
> - Improves the ability to cross the centerline and to turn the head left and right
> - Strengthens balance between the neck and upper shoulder muscles
> - Relaxes the neck and the muscles of the shoulder girdle as well as the jaw and shoulder muscles
> - Increases blood circulation and energy flow to the brain
> - Prevents over-extension and an incorrect tilt of the head when focusing

Fig. 24

The Correct Position of the Head, Neck, Shoulders and Arms

The shoulders should be square and in a natural position; ideally an observer can see a soft wrinkle in the back of the rider's shirt. The shoulder blades should not be sticking out in the back. The correct posture gives the look of an open chest that can easily receive lots of air in the lungs, but which is not stiff. The arms should hang softly at the rider's sides, with a bend in the elbow and the elbow slightly in front of the torso. There should be a straight line from the elbow to the bit, and the reins should be held correctly in the closed fingers (See Fig. 25). It should look like the rider is receiving energy in his hands, not holding it, or taking it back towards the abdomen.

COMMON DEVIATIONS IN THE HEAD, NECK, SHOULDERS AND ARMS

All the strengthening and stretching of various muscles is in vain if the head-neck-and-shoulder area is not relaxed. Our bodies were

Having a "flat pressed thumb" and a hard fist stiffen riders' wrists. The tension caused by this reaches all the way into the shoulder area. Having a bend in the thumbs and a relaxed but firm fist keep the wrist's range of motion intact.

Fig. 25

constructed in such a way that we are able to carry large burdens on our heads without difficulty. There are still tribes and groups of people today who can easily carry large loads on their heads without developing back problems. In our culture, however, we do not carry loads on our heads anymore, but rather *in* our heads—psychological loads. Many people today suffer from tension in the head-neck-and-shoulder area because of their psychological burdens.

I often hear from instructors that many of their students have tight shoulders and necks. In order to get rid of this tension, instructors (and students) must know that many different things usually cause tension in the upper body.

The Tilt of the Head
The tilt of the head can produce either a positive or a negative effect on a rider's motion. The way a rider sits can be compared to a ship's mast *(See Fig. 16, page 99)*. The slightest change somewhere in the body affects the rest of the body as well. As strange as it may seem, people tend to hold their heads a bit lopsided, caused by imbalances in the neck muscles. Just by carrying our heads at a slight tilt to the left or right we produce changes in our spine. If riders hold their heads slightly tilted to the right they will automatically sit more to the left in the saddle (and vice versa). Changes in the rider's center of gravity will not be symmetric because of the tilt of the head, and the horse will, therefore, not be able to maintain its balance either. Tilting the head to the front or back, which is less common, may result from using the head to try to balance stiffness elsewhere in the body.

Commands cannot solve these problems. If the instructor were to yell, "Head straight!" the rider would consciously hold his head up, but in such a way that his neck would get stiff and tight. This, in turn, would make his entire posture stiff and tight too. The head is directly connected to the pelvis by the spine. Therefore if the head is held in a fixed position, the pelvis will likewise be held in a fixed position, making smooth following of the horse's motion impossible.

The lopsided head posture can be improved by doing specific stretches for the neck and shoulder muscles. It is important that both sides of the neck be stretched, but the shortened side (the side that the head leans toward) should be stretched more.

Neck and Shoulder Tension

As I have mentioned earlier, the neck muscles and neck vertebrae are actually not strong enough to hold the head perfectly straight. In order to have a correct and natural neck posture, riders must do specific and intense exercises to strengthen their neck and shoulder muscles and to make them more supple.

Tension in the shoulders and neck can also be caused when riders clamp their legs onto the horse. Instructors may want their riders to use a little more leg strength to influence the horse and thus tell the rider to "close your legs" or knees. However, if instructors say this without any explanation their riders will likely exaggerate and clamp their legs onto the horse. The adductor muscles (the inside thigh muscles) then tense up and cause the shoulders and neck area to tense up also. Specifically the tension in the clamped adductors causes the pelvis to tilt backward, which causes the spine to curve. The chin automatically rises, which then causes the shoulders and neck muscles to tense up.

The commands to "close the legs" (or knees) and then, at the same time, to "stay loose in the shoulders" are simply impossible to follow. The human body is not a machine. It is an intricately connected and holistically functional organism. It is very important that both students and instructors understand that tension in one part of the body can have its source somewhere else in the body. Students should practice becoming "in tune" with their bodies and feeling where tensions are and where they originate. This will help them locate and fix problem areas more rapidly.

Besides having a natural tendency to tighten, the neck and shoulder muscles can be affected by the intensity of one's grip on the reins. If riders grip the reins with too much strength the arm muscles tighten, then the tension quickly works its way up the arms into the shoulders and neck.

Another cause for neck and shoulder tension is if the head is tilted either too far backward or forward. The muscles strain to hold this position and become tight. Incorrect posture of the head is often caused by an incorrect posture of the pelvis, as mentioned earlier. Therefore, if the shoulders are tight, it can mean that the pelvis is also tight.

This direct connection can be responsible for a slight bobbing of the head. Every time the tight pelvis hits against the saddle the jolt travels up the spine into the shoulders and causes the head to bob. However, if the pelvis is relaxed and free riders can better follow the rhythm and motion of the horse with smooth pelvic undulations and the neck no longer has to absorb the shock of the horse's motion. A relaxed yet firm hold of the reins lets the horse do his job without making him feel constrained. This also facilitates better communication between horse and rider.

EXERCISES FOR THE HEAD NECK, SHOULDERS, AND ARMS

Neck Swing

In addition to relaxing your neck, this exercise will improve your ability to work around and across the centerline of your body, and will help you to feel more centered. The motions also relax the neck muscles and release blockages, as well as relaxing the central nervous system, which controls the "alert status" of your entire body. Your breathing will improve and your whole body will relax.

Breathe rhythmically and calmly during this exercise. Your neck should not be strained or overly stretched either sideways or forward/backward because this will cause tension. When rolling your neck back you should have the feeling of still being able to swallow; that is, do not let your head fall so far back that your esophagus is compressed. Make sure that you are not lifting your shoulders to meet your ear, but instead are allowing the ear to come as close to the shoulder as it naturally can.

When you find a position where your neck feels particularly tense, just hold that position for a few moments until the tension is released. Your shoulders should also become more relaxed through this exercise. After the first few rolls, do the same exercises, but with your shoulders drawn up towards your ears, and then repeat again with your shoulders hanging relaxed. Experiment also with doing these exercises with eyes open or eyes closed and see if you can feel a difference. Make sure never to let your head "drop;" always hold it lightly in position while rolling.

Starting Position: Look straight ahead.

Movement: Use very slow and smooth (not jerky or quick) motions throughout this exercise. Roll your neck in the following directions ONLY: Begin by allowing your head to hang forward with your chin moving towards your sternum. From this position gently roll your right ear towards your right shoulder, then roll it down to the center again, and then roll your left ear towards your left shoulder. Repeat several times, then lift your head up again so that it is over your neck. From this position roll your head slowly forward towards your chest and then backwards so that your eyes look up at the sky.

Important: NEVER ROLL YOUR HEAD IN CIRCLES!

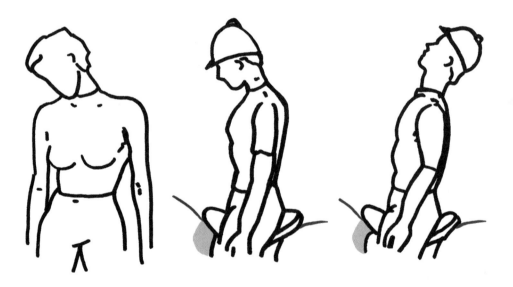

Fig. 26

IMPORTANT NOTE REGARDING STRETCHING/LENGTHENING MUSCLES

Do not bounce when you stretch or lengthen your muscles; instead, slowly push yourself to your length limit. The length limit is the point at which you just begin to feel pain. It is important not to go past this point. Hold the stretch for about 10 seconds at your length limit. The pain that you feel is a sign that your muscle is protecting itself from being torn. The "extension" reflex, preventing further stretching, sets in at this point, but releases after about 10 seconds of immobility. After the reflex has released, you can stretch the muscle a little bit farther. The first phase is simply easy lengthening (stretching). The second phase is where the muscle actually becomes more supple. Be sure to only stretch gently, concentrating on feeling your muscles being lengthened. Never force anything to stretch. Lengthening one muscle can take up to two minutes or more.

Lengthening the Throat and Neck Muscles

Starting position: Stand with your feet slightly apart (straddled).

Movements: Your left hand reaches over your head and holds your head near your right temple. Then you slowly pull your head to the left to its maximum extension, while, at the same time, stretching your right arm as far towards the ground as possible. Follow the rules for stretching/lengthening muscles, and then repeat on the other side.

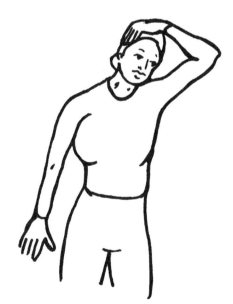

Fig. 27

(For more exercises see *Exercise Program for Riders,* Meyners 2003)

The Correct Position of the Torso

The spine connects the head, arms and pelvis, and is the vehicle for communication between them. Each joint must be upright and yet flexible. Each of the vertebrae offers some movement that allows the overall outward appearance of no movement. A flat "S" shape of the spine supports upright posture, which is long and tall without being held. The actual form of the spine is impossible to see without x-ray vision, but only a correctly aligned spine can provide the correct elasticity needed to maintain the ideal posture and to use the effective driving aids *(See Fig. 11, page 96).*

COMMON DEVIATIONS OF THE TORSO
Slouching
Instead of sitting vertically and straight, some riders tend to sit with their chest caved in and their shoulders hunched. This makes them lean forward a little. It is not done on purpose, but is simply a bad habit that is difficult to break. It is important to know some physiological and anatomical background in this situation. The pectoral muscles across the chest tend to shorten, thus making riders sit "caved in" or stooped forward. The opposing muscles, those of the shoulder girdle, tend to be weak and cannot oppose the strong pectorals. Riders can only straighten up with a conscious effort, but they fall right back into their bad posture once they turn their attention back to the horse. Therefore riders who strain to sit upright usually become stiff and cramped.

The Open Seat
An open seat results when riders are not able to sit with their shoulders and hips parallel to those of the horse. Instead they sit with their shoulders pulled back stiffly, and do not allow any twist in their spines. The ability to turn the spine in response to the bend in the horse's spine is essential for having an effective dialogue with the horse. In order to "close" the seat, the rider must bring his inner hip forward and down (towards the knee on that side) so that the outer oblique stomach muscles pull the outer shoulder forward. If the rider only thinks of bringing the inside hip forward (without also thinking down towards the knee), the inside shoulder will be

pulled forward instead of the outside shoulder and the rider will continue in the open seat.

The Crooked Seat

A sideways curvature of the spine as well as weaker lumbar musculature on one side can also cause an unbalanced seat. Having symmetrical oblique stomach muscles keeps our upper body in an upright position and does not allow it to lean to one side. Most people have a stronger and weaker side to these muscles, resulting in a degree of leaning. The weaker side must be strengthened to counteract the muscular imbalance.

— EXERCISES FOR THE TORSO —

Arm Flow

Babies and toddlers have very supple sternums because the crawling motion keeps that area loose. As adults, people's sternums become stabilized and rigid due to lack of use and movement. This tension also affects the entire neck-shoulder area. When a person is able to release the sternum, the neck and shoulder area will also become relaxed.

Starting position: Hold your arm out at shoulder level, with the elbow slightly bent and the hand hanging limply from the wrist, so that your hand is about a foot in front of your nose.

Movement: Gently move your arm outward from the shoulder away from your body, and turn your head in the opposite direction. Repeat this a few times with each arm. Next, take your arm from the starting position and move it towards the opposite shoulder, again turning your head in the opposite direction. When you are using your right arm, as you take your arm outward to the right, your head should turn left, and as you take your arm toward the left shoulder across your centerline your head should turn right. After a few repetitions you will be able look more easily over your shoulder.

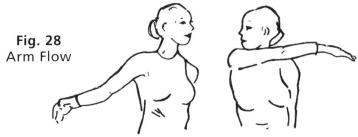

Fig. 28
Arm Flow

IMPORTANT NOTE REGARDING STRENGTHENING MUSCLES

Muscle strengthening is most effective when done using either a stationary or a slowly dynamic position so that all the muscle fibers are worked on. Make sure not to allow any jerky movements when using the muscle. Jerky movements prevent the muscle from being strengthened at its full length. Instead only the middle of the muscle will become strengthened, which inhibits the effectiveness of that muscle. This is why body builders with very strong biceps may not be able to straighten their arms completely. To strengthen your muscles in a stationary position move SLOWLY into the strengthening position and hold it for 8 to 10 seconds. It is important to keep breathing while you are holding the position! SLOWLY return to the starting position. There are two ways to increase the weight strain (strength level): 1) Increase the amount of time that the strengthening position is held, from 10 seconds up to 30 seconds, and 2) Increase the number of repetitions so that you hold the position for 8 to 10 seconds several times in succession (up to 15 repetitions) with 10 to 20 second breaks in between. The number of repetitions depends on your own personal fitness. Be sure to keep breathing when moving from the starting position into the new position.

Strengthening the Oblique Stomach Muscles

Starting position (without a partner): Lie on your back with your hips and knees at 90 degree angles, so that your feet are off the ground.

Movements: Interlock your fingers and reach your joined hands past your right thigh, lifting the left shoulder and torso off of the ground. Repeat taking the joined hands past the left thigh (Fig. 29).

Starting position (with a partner): Lie on your back with your knees bent and your feet flat on the floot. Have a partner brace himself on your knee and place his left palm against your left palm.

Movements: Lift your torso up in the direction of your partner's hand, pressing your partner's hand away from you. Repeat on the other side (Fig. 30).

RIDER — Effective Teaching & Riding   113

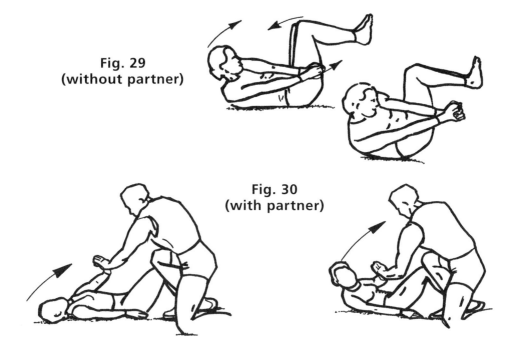

Fig. 29 (without partner)

Fig. 30 (with partner)

Lengthening the Middle Chest Muscles

Starting position: Sit cross-legged. Hold your arms out at your sides at shoulder level and bend them at the elbow so that your hands reach toward the ceiling.

Movements: Have a partner gently pull your arms backwards, keeping your upper arms at shoulder level.

Important: Do not arch your back. Be sure to stabilize your pelvis.

Fig. 31

Lengthening the Lower Chest Muscles

Starting position: Sit cross-legged. Hold your arms out at your sides at shoulder level and bend them at the elbow so that your hands reach toward the ceiling.

Movements: Have your partner gently pull your arms backwards and upward. Allow your arms to straighten as needed. This exercise will help prevent slouching.

Important: Do not arch your back. Be sure to stabilize your pelvis.

Fig. 32

Strengthening the Muscles on the Side of the Torso (in the loin area)

Starting position: Lie on your side with both legs out straight (it is ok if your knees are bent a little bit). Place the top leg on the floor a little in front of the bottom leg. Place your arms straight out in front of your body, with the palms touching. Your head should be in line with your spine.

Movements: Lift your upper body off of the floor, using the muscles on the sides of your body. You may need a partner to hold your feet flat on the floor.

A variation of this exercise includes lifting your arms off of the floor at the same time as your torso. This exercise should be done on both sides, while taking care to strengthen the weaker side more.

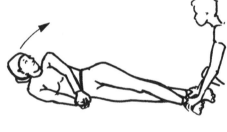

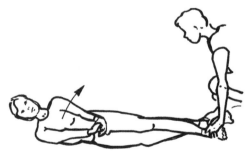

Fig. 33

Strengthening the Back Muscles

Starting position: Lie on your stomach. Put a folded hand towel or blanket under your stomach. Interlace your hands behind your head.

Movements: Slightly lift your upper body and legs off the floor, while keeping your neck straight by looking at the floor.

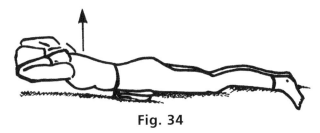

Fig. 34

Strengthening the Back Muscles

Starting position: Lie on your stomach. Put a folded hand towel or blanket under your stomach. Stretch your arms out straight over your head.

Movements: Slowly raise your arms and legs, keeping your neck straight and eyes looking at the floor.

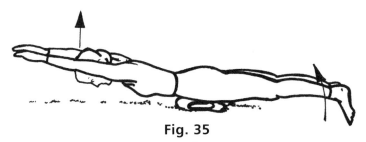

Fig. 35

Strengthening the Back Muscles, Buttock Muscles and the Back of the Thighs

Starting Position: Lie on your stomach. Put a folded hand towel or blanket under your stomach. Stretch your arms out straight over your head.

Movements: Lift only your legs off the floor and tighten your buttock muscles.

Fig. 36

> **Strengthening the Stomach Muscles, Especially the Lower Stomach Muscles.**
>
> **Starting position:** Lie on your back with your knees bent, the soles of your feet on the floor, and your arms on the floor by your sides.
> **Movements:** Bring your thighs and knees towards your chest and lift your buttocks off the ground.

Fig. 37

The Correct Position of the Pelvis

The pelvis is the most important multipurpose hinge for the rider. It consists of three very important joints: the ilio-sacral joint, which connects the pelvis to the spine; and the two hip joints, which connect each hip to the corresponding thigh bone. The pelvis is also the rider's base of support. The three joints of the pelvis must be as flexible as possible in order to follow the horse's motion and to impart effective aids. It is important for riders to select horses whose width is comfortable for their pelvis. Riders with narrow hips need a narrow horse, while riders with wider hips will fit more comfortably on a wider horse. It is also important for a rider to avoid excess flesh in the buttocks as this interferes with the movement of the pelvis and the dialogue with the horse.

COMMON DEVIATIONS OF THE PELVIS
A Blocked or Stiff Ilio-Sacral (IS) Joint

Even when riders' muscles are balanced and function smoothly, they might still have problems following the horse's motion if the ilio-sacral joint is blocked. Most back pain is caused by problems within this joint. When this joint is blocked, it is not possible for riders to have 3-dimensional motions in their bod-

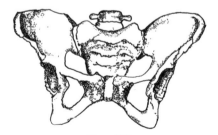

Fig. 38
Ilio-Sacral (IS) Joint

ies. Since all of our motions when riding are 3-dimensional, if the ilio-sacral joint is blocked it is not possible for riders to follow the motion of the horse.

Two bones that are joined by tendons define a joint. The IS-joint consists of the tailbone (the last 5 vertebrae which have fused together) and its connection to the pelvic ring (Fig. 38).

Not only is blockage of the pelvis a problem in horseback riding, it is also a problem most people have in general. Bad posture and the resulting shortening or lengthening of pelvic muscles are usually the cause of common back pain and muscle aches. Muscles that are prone to shorten, such as muscles in the back, greatly influence the function and health of the pelvis. Stomach muscles that should work against the shortening of the back muscles are prone to weakness and need to be strengthened.

A Rounded Back

Some riders sit with their hips (pelvis) tilted back and their knees pulled upward and clamped too tightly onto the horse. This is often referred to as a "chair" seat. When the hips are tilted backward, the knees are pulled up automatically. By straightening the hips the knees automatically go down and the rider sits straighter in the saddle. Instructors should make sure that they correct the rider's hips before they try to correct the legs or knees.

Fig. 39

The Hollow Back

If the legs are too straight (tensed), riders will not be able to feel or sense the horse's motions or give the right aids. This may also result in tilting the pelvis forward and arching the lower back, which is seen as a "hollow back." Riders need to strengthen the buttocks and back muscles and the stomach muscles while lengthening the hip adductors (inner hip benders) to acquire better posture in the saddle. *(See torso exercises pge 111 and leg exercises page 123.)*

— EXERCISES FOR THE PELVIS —

Shoulder-Knee Stretch

This stretch helps to unblock the IS-joint. This usually feels very good to riders and has an immediate impact on both horse and rider.

Starting Position: Lie on your back with one leg straight and one knee bent with the sole of that foot on the ground.

Movement: Your partner gently presses the bent leg over the straight leg while holding onto the shoulder to be sure that it does not come off the ground. The foot is allowed to come off the ground. The bend in the knee can vary so that the knee comes close to or touches the ground at various places as your partner continues to gently press the knee towards the ground. Usually you will feel varying amounts of tension in the IS-joint as this is being done. It is important to relax and allow your partner to do the work rather than tensing up against the motion.

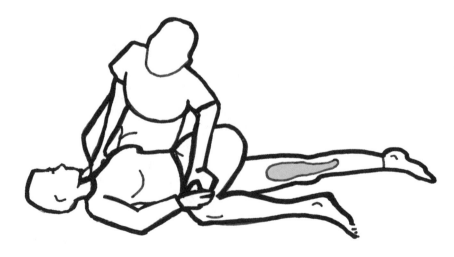

Fig.40

Crawl to a Sitting Position

By using this exercise riders can make sure that their ilio-sacral joint is not blocked.

When a person goes from all fours to a sitting position the lower back arches because the head leans back on the neck (the incorrect position of head-neck-shoulders-spine). However by tilting the head down toward the chest the back is curved and not arched. When the motions of the head and pelvis are combined the entire motion becomes more elastic and lighter. By crossing one leg in front of the other this (correct) curve of the spine is intensified and carried forward into the sitting position.

Fig. 41

Lengthening the Hip Adductors (*clamping* muscles)

Starting position: Sit on the floor with one leg straight and the other leg bent at the knee. Spread your legs and hold the ankle of the bent leg with the hand on the same side, keeping your arms inside your knees.

Movements: Press the bent knee outward.

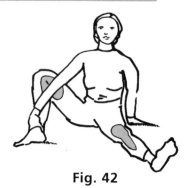

Fig. 42

Lengthening the Hip Adductors (*clamping* muscles)

Starting position: Sit on the floor with your back straight. Put the soles of your feet together with your feet as close to your body as possible.

Movements: Slowly let your knees fall toward the floor. With your hands on your knees, press your elbows toward the floor, making your knees sink closer to the floor.

Fig. 43

Lengthening the Hip Adductors (*clamping* muscles)

Starting position: Sit on the floor with your legs straight and spread apart as far as possible. Place both hands flat on the floor in front of you, keeping your back straight.

Movements: Bend forward with your upper body, including your pelvis. Make sure that you "hinge" at the hips and not at the waist. Only go as far forward as is comfortable or possible without collapsing at the waist.

Important: Do not let your pelvis tip backward or round your back.

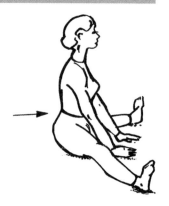

Fig. 44

RIDER — Effective Teaching & Riding 121

Clock

A good exercise that can help prevent incorrect tilting of the pelvis and a hollow back is rolling the pelvis in all directions. This can be done first in a sitting position on the Balimo chair (*See Appendix for more information*) to get used to the motions, and then, once students have a feel for the rolling motions and can do them correctly, they can begin to loosen these muscles while on the horse.

The rolling motion should always be done slowly and carefully. Students should imagine their pelvis sitting on the face of a clock. When they tilt their pelvis backwards it is at 6:00. By tilting the pelvis forward they arrive at 12:00. A tilt towards the left knee is 10:00 (this is the aid for a left lead canter), and a tilt toward the right knee is 2:00 (and also the aid for a right lead canter). Starting at 12:00 riders can roll their pelvis clockwise and counterclockwise around the face of the clock .

While rolling either clockwise or counterclockwise, students will be able to feel that certain positions (or, in this case, "hours") are not very easy to reach or hold. It is important that in these more difficult positions students do not tense or overexert to the point of pain. After rolling the pelvis smoothly and slowly without force "around the clock" many times students will notice that the positions that were difficult at first become much easier and that the muscles involved in this exercise loosen up.

This "rolling around the clock" exercise helps students feel the connection between head and pelvis and helps them realize what it means and feels like to sit up straight. By tilting toward 12:00 in the saddle, riders grow taller and the chin falls down toward the

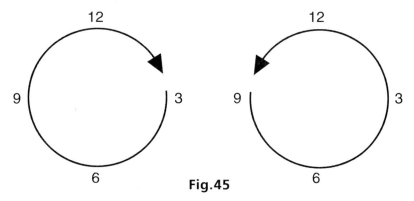

Fig.45

chest. If the pelvis is tilted toward 6:00 the chin rises away from the chest. This exercise shows students that the position of their pelvis directly influences the position of their head through their spine. Afterwards riders will feel taller and straighter in the saddle. Both students and instructors should understand that in order to straighten up in the saddle, the pelvis must be positioned correctly. It is important for each rider to find his or her own optimal pelvic position in the saddle.

The Correct Position of the Legs

The rider's conformation plays an important role in finding the correct leg position. A rider with a long, flat thigh with little excess flesh has the ideal conformation to have an effective leg position and use of the aids. The leg, from the hip joint downward, needs to become longer while the body from the hips upward grows taller, without tension. The ideal thigh should rest on the saddle like an uncooked sirloin steak, with the knee resting softly against the saddle so that it can act as a shock absorber. The back of the calf is softly in contact with the horse's sides, and the foot rests in the stirrup on the ball so that the ankle (the most important shock absorber) can spring up and down with the horse's motion.

COMMON DEVIATIONS IN THE LEGS
Heels
A very common deviation seen in the leg is a drawn-up heel. Often neither the rider nor the instructor understands the reason behind this deviation from the ideal, softly springing ankle and heel. This lack of understanding is obviously why instructors yell, "Toes up!" or "Heels down!" The rider's heel position results from the position of the rest of the rider's body, so it is rarely effective to try to directly correct a heel position. It is far more effective to look elsewhere in the rider's body for a blockage or stiffness and make the correction there. The rider's heel will reflect this change. High heel position is also commonly caused by incorrectly applied driving aids.

Driving aids
Many riders are not aware of how to correctly drive a horse forward, and therefore do not understand how to hold their legs and heels

correctly. Driving correctly, by using one's hamstrings, automatically brings the heels down. Incorrect driving uses the calf muscles (behind the knee joint) or the adductors instead of the hamstrings, which is observed in the resulting drawn-up heel. If the hamstrings are not used to drive correctly, the calf muscles jump into action. If riders are not sure of their balance or are experiencing any fear, they may grip the horse with their adductors, which also prevents correct driving. To avoid using the wrong muscles students must consciously use their hamstrings.

When riders tense their hamstring muscles, their knees automatically bend and their calves come close to the horse's sides. This is done rhythmically (tensing the hamstring and loosening, then repeating as needed) with the motion of the horse. Riders who have weak hamstrings must see to it that they strengthen and stretch them.

In order to apply the hamstring muscles correctly the stirrups cannot be too long. Riders should not have to reach down too much with their legs or toes. They must be relaxed and balanced. If the stirrups are too long, the calf muscles automatically become tense, drawing up the heels.

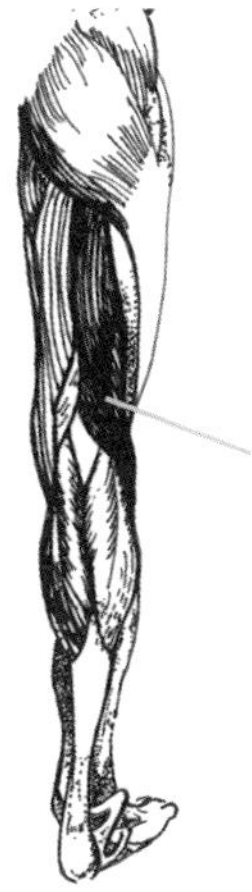

**Fig. 46
Hamstrings**

— EXERCISES FOR THE LEGS —

Developing Awareness of the Hamstrings

It may be important for riders to experience the proper driving muscles while off the horse before trying to find and coordinate them on the horse. This can be accomplished by having the rider lie on her stomach on a mat, and then bend one leg at the knee. A helper should then provide some resistance with his hand on the back of the rider's leg as she performs this movement. The helper can watch her foot position as she bends her leg. If she is using her calf muscles, the toe will point, but if she is using her hamstrings correctly, the toe will lift towards the shin as she bends her leg at the knee. Through experimentation the rider will discover which muscles to use in order to drive the horse correctly. Once she has felt this feeling, she is then ready to try it on the horse.

Strengthening the Back of the Thighs and Buttock Muscles.

Starting position: Lie on your back with your knees and hips at 90 degree angles to each other, resting your heels on a chair and supporting your upper body with your elbows.

Movements: Lift your buttocks off the floor

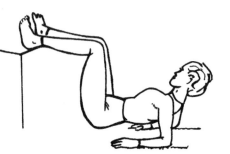

Fig. 47

Lengthening the Back of the Thighs (Hamstrings) and the Calves

Starting position: Stand up straight and place your heel on a chair in front of you. Cross your arms behind your back.

Movements: Flex your toes toward your shin as far as possible, and then slowly lean forward with your pelvis and upper body, bending at the hips rather than at the waist.

Additional Influences on the Rider's Seat

The rider's overall seat is influenced by the specific positions and motions of individual body parts, but there are other factors which influence the seat and the whole sense of motion. The rider is only able to sit on the horse in a manner that reflects her motions and postures in the rest of her life. These additional influences on the development of each rider's seat are discussed below.

Fig. 48

UNMOUNTED POSTURE AND THE CORRECT SEAT

There is a direct connection between our posture and the energy flow in our bodies. Bad posture causes disturbances in our body energies and produces stress. Biologists have learned that upright posture (balancing on two legs) is much more efficient than balancing on four legs. Animals must use 40% of their energy to stay balanced on their four legs, while humans only have to use 18% of their energy to stay balanced. This 18%, however, refers only to people whose posture reflects maximum efficiency. Many people have bad posture habits, such as hunched shoulders or protruding heads and they will expend more energy to remain upright. Horseback riders who have bad posture not only look bad, but they also use more energy than is necessary. Instead of using gravity to their advantage, they constantly fight against it.

Bad posture has a negative effect on the entire body. There are particular parts of the body that are especially affected, for example, the thymus gland. The importance of the thymus was not well known until recent new studies showed that the thymus gland has direct connections to stress and the development of certain serious diseases (crib death, chronic illness, disturbances in the immune system, infection, cancer, etc.). The human thymus gland is located in the middle of the chest directly behind the upper part of the breastbone (or sternum). Bad posture (in our daily lives and on a horse) weakens the function of the thymus gland, damaging our energy systems.

Not only does bad posture have negative effects on the thymus gland but it also affects our brains. Bad posture can lead to what is called "switching." The left side of the brain normally controls the right side of the body and the right side of the brain normally controls the left side of the body by sending messages across the corpus callosum, which is the connection point between the two brain hemispheres. When this communication cannot take place, "switching" occurs. This is a condition in which the body is confused and a person is not centered because the two sides of the brain are not equally balanced. The result is homolateral motion. You can observe homolateral motion in a person who is walking when their left arm and leg advance together and then their right arm and leg advance together instead of the normal cross-coordinated motion where the left leg and the right arm swing forward together and then the right leg and the left arm swing forward. "Switching" is a particularly stressful situation for the body.

Bad Posture = Stress

We know that bad posture in daily activities and on a horse produces stress in the body. Making artificial changes in our posture will not help avoid this, nor will it solve the real problem. "Artificial" means that these changes are only external, forced and short-term. We must make real, long-term changes in our daily posture and daily activities. These changes must be self-initiated and result from changes inside the body rather than changes to the body's external form.

Activities that lead to "switching" should (and can) be avoided in day-to-day life. Here are a few examples: bicycling (when cross-coordination exercises are not done afterwards), sitting on hard metal chairs or soft couches, bad car seats, desk chairs, etc. Furthermore, some on-the-job situations put our bodies under constant stress. The postures required of dentists, barbers or hairdressers and salesclerks, for example, also lead to "switching." Wearing high-heeled shoes is also a major cause of "switching." People from these career fields will have a difficult time finding smooth coordination and undulating motion on a horse due to the enormous amount of physical stress caused by their job. This on-the-job stress could be a reason why some people are never able to learn to feel (or have a dialogue with) the horse. There are practical exercises designed to help people learn to balance their energies on the horse and in daily life which are described throughout this book. *(See, crawling, sideways figure 8, elephant.)*

Bad Habits in Daily Posture

Our daily motion habits as modern humans are not equal to the motions that we are *actually* capable of. Adults have forgotten motions that children are still able to perform and have learned bad habits that de-sensitized our ability to feel our bodies and to feel our own correct posture.

Before riders can learn how to feel (on and with) the horse, they must first learn to have better posture and more fluid motions in daily life. Only after they have learned to constantly be aware of their own body and their own posture can they begin to learn how to feel slight changes in the horse's motion. Therefore, learning to *feel* must begin with everyday motions.

The following figures illustrate incorrect postures that are caused by misbalanced muscles.

A rider with an arched back bends the knees, but the hips fail to function as hinges. Because the head-neck-and-back muscles shorten the rider is not relaxed and cannot undulate with the horse's rhythm. The rider's motion constantly counters the horse's motion.

Fig. 49A

A rider who has a rounded back instead of an arched back. A rounded back causes similar problems with maintaining rhythm and motion with the horse.

Fig. 49b

The normal but incorrect posture of a person who is brushing her teeth. Her knees are locked, her head protrudes out in front, and her pelvis is tilted forward so that her belly sticks out. This posture is far from being elastic and supple—it is rigid. Having good posture in the saddle will be nearly impossible if this kind of bad posture is not corrected beforehand.

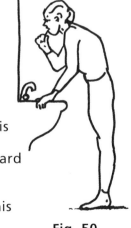

Fig. 50

Fig. 51
A normal and easy posture for a child, showing balance and flexibility.

Fig. 52
A normal sitting posture we all had to begin with!

Young children move freely and fluidly and still have perfectly relaxed and natural postures

However, during childhood the negative influences of our environment have such an effect on a child's nervous system that over time it becomes so overwhelmed that it cannot automatically counter these effects.

The child is totally relaxed as he bends down to pick up an object. His entire muscle system is balanced. When children sit anywhere their entire muscular system is relaxed and they do not get stiff. Adults have somehow forgotten these relaxed motions and movements. When adults sit or bend down for something they no longer use the correct muscles or the correct posture, and this leads to stiffness and pain.

Fig. 53

Animals, however, maintain a natural posture throughout their lives: the head leads and the body follows.

Fig. 54

Typical Posture Habits in Adults

Bad posture habits most adults have in their everyday motions.

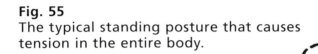

Fig. 55
The typical standing posture that causes tension in the entire body.

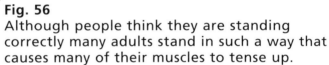

Fig. 56
Although people think they are standing correctly many adults stand in such a way that causes many of their muscles to tense up.

This habit of incorrect standing posture makes it nearly impossible to develop a good and elastic seat. When people with bad posture are supposed to sit "naturally" in the saddle, they will likely return to the habitually bad posture of their everyday lives. Any corrections from the instructor will feel unnatural to them because they are so accustomed to the bad posture.

Figure 57 depicts a very typical posture for adult riders. These riders seem to be relaxed, and they do not feel any negative stimuli from their body. However, their posture deviates greatly from the natural sitting posture.

Crossing one's legs while sitting in a chair only makes this bad posture worse. It shortens the adductor muscles in the legs and prevents the pelvic muscles from being elastic. The adductors directly influence the neck and shoulder muscles. When one's adductor

Fig. 57
Relaxed but incorrect postures

muscles are tight or shortened, one's neck and shoulder muscles will also become tight.

Habitual bad posture prevents riders from being able to feel or sense natural body tone and impedes their ability to straighten up into a natural posture.

Bad Posture at a Desk

Writing at a desk causes the back to curve, which causes the spine and the entire body to suffer as well (Fig. 58). Breathing problems may occur, along with loss of rhythm in motions, which is directed by breathing. These breathing problems are caused by pressure on the chest. The brain "remembers" this posture and recalls it when a person sits on a horse. A curved spine and the backward tilt of the pelvis make it impossible to use changes in one's center of gravity for aids (the "weight" aids).

Fig. 58

"Steering" with the Head

A person with bad posture during childhood and the teen years will carry this muscle tension on with him into adulthood.

Fig. 59
Head sunken into neck

The head sinks further down onto the neck (Fig. 58), which causes lower back pain and intensifies an arched back in the lumbar region. A rider with this type of bad posture will not be able to undulate smoothly with the horse because this posture blocks the occipital joint (between the base of the skull and the first neck vertebra).

Since the head "steers" the entire body, bad posture often begins with the head. It then flows over into the neck region and on into the torso.

Fig. 60 Illustrates how tension in the large neck muscles leads to tension throughout the body.

Even incorrect posture while standing up causes problems with the entire musculature. The way we adults get up from a sitting position (for example, out of a chair) is one of the worst things we do to ourselves. Our necks are stiff, our heads fall back on our necks, our chests protrude forward, our backs are over-extended and our rear ends are stuck out. It does not get any worse than that! Over years and years of getting up incorrectly we slowly damage our bodies in very acute ways.

STANDING CORRECTLY

Although children are still growing accustomed to their own bodies, they have a naturally correct posture. However, the modern age has radically changed our standing postures for the worse.

The musculature system is not balanced in figure 61A, causing compensation by tilting the pelvis forward. The lumbar region of the spine must then deal with enormous pressure, which, of course, has effects on the rest of the muscles; everything is under pressure and tight. Even the seemingly "relaxed" standing posture illustrated in figure 61B does not allow all muscles

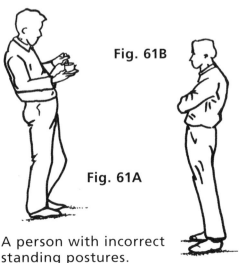

Fig. 61B

Fig. 61A

A person with incorrect standing postures.

in the body to really relax. This hunched back posture (hips and belly jutted forward) causes tiredness and puts strain on the inner organs.

"Stand up straight!" is a typical command that we all hear more than once in our lifetimes. Because most people do not know how to correctly stand up straight, they over-exaggerate in response to this command and cause more muscular imbalances.

The person in figure 62 thinks he is standing correctly, although his body is obviously crooked and tense.

Often in riding lessons students are told to sit up straight. They try their best to follow these instructions. However, instead of sitting straight and relaxed, they tense up because they do not know **how** to correctly sit up straight. They use the wrong muscles, resulting in more stress and less comfort for horse and rider. Many riders also try to sit straight as illustrated in figure 63. This strained posture only leads to complete tension in all of the riders' motions. These riders sit extremely straight, as though they had swallowed a broomstick.

Fig. 62
A typical example of how inadequate our senses are in perceiving our own bodies.

Fig. 63
Rider trying to sit straight in saddle

Fig. 64
Cogwheel

Getting to the point of correctly sitting straight is a slow process. The cogwheel example (Fig. 64) helps students to straighten themselves correctly. When the pelvis is rolled forward the chest automatically fills out, the shoulders fall back and, because the neck vertebrae extend, the chin also drops toward the chest, creating naturally balanced straightness.

WALKING IS THE SAME AS RIDING!
Although this idea may seem silly or impossible, it is absolutely correct. Riders tend to constantly sit crooked; their center of gravity shifts with every step of the horse. For example, more weight is put on the left seat bone and the right shoulder tenses a little in response. The same thing occurs when we walk. When the right leg swings forward the left shoulder and arm should swing forward, too. This is called *cross-coordinated motion*. Many people today do not swing their arms fully or let their hips and shoulders turn naturally. Often this results when babies skip crawling and move directly from sitting to walking. Crawling provides invaluable experience with cross-coordination that is essential for mental and physical development. These people would have difficulties on a horse as well because their shoulders would not turn when the horse's shoulders turn. Both on a horse and walking on the ground, the spine needs to twist with each step. This is necessary for proper brain functioning (communication across the hemispheres) as well as for being in proper rhythm and harmony with the horse.

We can also guess by the way a person walks if they would tend to clamp onto the horse with their legs or to sit too "open." People who tend to turn their toes inward have very strong adductor muscles and would not be able to undulate smoothly on a horse. If their toes are turned outward when walking, they would also turn outward on a horse, causing their knees to turn out as well. This inhibits smooth rhythmic motions with the horse. Generally speaking, we can say that if a person has a smooth, flexible walking gait they will also be able to ride a horse smoothly and flexibly.

Instructors Beware! Instructors must be very careful in their corrections because everything they correct has an effect on the rest of the rider's body. If a rider over corrects in a particular area the instructor will sooner or later have to correct somewhere else. This can go on and on. Therefore, instructors must not only make sure that their students understand how their own bodies function so that they can better understand how to correct themselves, but they must also be aware that the corrections they make to a student's position have a profound effect on that student's posture. This process begins with identifying the deviations that need to be corrected. Most of the time the place where the correction is needed is not the place where it is visible. If a rider is sitting with slumped shoulders, this is more likely to be the result of a problem in the pelvis or neck than it is with the shoulders. Instructors need to be very familiar with the interconnections in the human body and help riders learn to feel these connections so the riders can identify the root of any deviations from the ideal that occur. Riders' seats are not only dependent on their position and posture but also on their horse and saddle and the surrounding environment as well as their own mental processes.

DYNAMIC MOTION OF THE HORSE

Instructors must work with each individual student on their posture to find the seat that is correct for them. The horse's dynamic motion has a great influence on this process.

The law of masses, from physics, is also very relevant for horseback riding; the larger mass always moves the smaller mass. Therefore, the smaller mass (the rider) must be able to become one with the larger mass (the horse) in order to get anywhere at all. Riders can use all kinds of aids, have good posture and a good seat, but if the horse does not "fit" with their body it will be very nearly impossible for any teamwork to happen (i.e. riders will not be able to sit correctly or influence the horse in an effective manner). For example, some horses have a very bumpy gait that jolts their riders around. Many riders have trouble getting used to the dynamic motion of these horses. Therefore, it is very important that a horse's energy and motion is compatible with that of its rider.

THE RIDER'S PROPORTIONS

The horse's size should match the rider's size. If a rider's legs are too long or too short for the horse, he will not be able to be effective. Too long is when the rider's foot falls well below the horse's flank, near the ground; too short is when the rider's foot falls in the middle of the horse's flank—these riders sit "on top of" the horse.

The width of a horse's back is also important. If the horse's back is too narrow, the rider's legs will be too close together, the adductor muscles will not be able to function properly, and the rider will have extreme difficulties following the horse's rhythm. The same goes for a horse with a back that is too wide for its rider. These riders sit "on top of" the horse with their legs stretched so wide that the pelvis and hips become totally blocked. Riders and horses are both unique creatures, and they must be matched with care and respect for their individual personalities and physical structure in order for a dialogue between the horse's back and the rider's seat to happen. Learning horsemanship and horseback riding is one of the most difficult sports exactly because the chemistry and physics between horse and rider must be so well matched.

SADDLE FIT

The question of finding the right saddle is just as difficult as finding the right rider and horse combination. Over the past decades the saddle gullet has grown smaller and smaller, and the resulting negative effects on the horse have been ignored. Saddles play a vital role in the dialogue between horse and rider because the saddle is the only thing connecting the two creatures. This problem can be solved, however, if competent saddle makers, veterinarians and equine physical therapists become involved. In this section I will not discuss the effect saddles have on horses, but rather I will concentrate on the effect saddles have in regard to riders.

Narrower saddles have been made to compensate for the growing tendency among riders to have shortened adductor muscles. These shortened adductors are caused by today's many stress factors; for example, sitting too long without moving one's legs, tilting the pelvis backward (arched back posture) and hunching one's shoulders.

Psychological stress also causes tightness in the muscle triangle between the shoulders and the head. This area is connected neuro-physiologically (by bundles of nerves) with the adductors.

Shortened adductors hinder riders' smoothness of motion. By making the saddles to compensate for this problem, we have only made the situation worse. Instead of making riders stretch these muscles, we made narrower saddles to compensate for their lack of flexibility, which means that the tension remains in both the adductors and the shoulders and head.

As a general rule, saddles must be compatible to the size of a person's seat. Riders should not "slip and slide" in their saddles. Conversely if a saddle is too small, it inhibits a rider's ability to engage with the horse's motion. It is also important that saddle flaps be adapted to fit the rider's leg structure.

Saddles with too much padding in front of and behind the legs seem to be "in." A large number of riders are delighted with these saddles because they are of the opinion that one can sit more comfortably. Although they may sit more comfortably, they sit too comfortably and are actually jammed into their saddle. If riders sit like this, they cannot engage with the horse's motion or influence the horse effectively. The orthopedic aids that are built into many saddles do not help riders; they only compensate for weak muscles. Riders do not learn how to balance by being jammed into their saddles, clamping their legs onto the horse's sides and sitting stiffly in the saddle. To learn balance riders need to be able to *move*, to discover the correct interaction of muscles that keeps them balanced and relaxed. Only then can they smoothly follow the horse's rhythm with their pelvis (in other words, undulate correctly and effectively with the horse's motion).

RELAXATION

Riders need to find an appropriate level of toned relaxation in their bodies and minds so that they can help their horses to find that same balance. A horse and rider who are relaxed, yet with the necessary muscle tone engaged, are ready for any type of performance task or learning challenge that may be presented to them. Interfering tension can come from the mind or the body. There are several very simple exercises you can use to achieve the appropriate level of relaxation.

— EXERCISES TO RELAX THE RIDER —

Smiling

The instructor can have a negative effect or a positive effect on the atmosphere simply by changing his or her facial expression. A smile creates a relaxed, positive atmosphere, whereas a frown creates a tense, negative atmosphere. The instructor's mood is contagious for the rider, and the rider's mood is contagious for the horse. It is important to know that a frown negatively affects the thymus gland, which conveys that negative message to the muscles, creating tension. When the face is pulled into a frown, it is felt in the occipital joint and the posture of the head, putting it out of centered alignment with the rest of the body. Kinesiology research has determined that this connection between a "centered head" and the rest of the body plays a major role in the harmony and function of the entire body.

A smile also offers positive reinforcement and creates a successful learning environment. Students who feel good about themselves and feel comfortable in their environment will be the most receptive to learning. For example, if a student walks into a room to take an exam and faces a room full of professors with scowls and frowns on their faces, the poor student immediately begins to think negatively, which can be seen physically in either a red face or a pale face. This student has a much lower chance of success than another student who walks into a room of smiling and friendly faces. All creatures can sense negative energy. This negative energy is difficult to diffuse. If people have high positive energy and let this show they can influence others in a wonderful manner. Smiling is one way to diffuse negative energy or to transform it into positive energy. Even if you are not feeling positive on the inside, if you put a smile on your face, your body picks up those signals and begins to put out different chemicals so that soon you even feel more positive.

Humming

Humming has two functions: 1) It re-establishes the body's natural vibrations and oscillations, and 2) It protects the body from stress. Riders who hum will find that their actions are much smoother and they are able to swing with the horse better. Humming also often allows riders to remember an action, which they had momentarily forgotten due to stress. This is a common scenario, especially for competition riders. We may forget how to do a specific action or perhaps the route of a jump course even though moments before we had it mastered. Humming can help riders remain in touch with all parts of themselves during a performance or any other stressful situation. Singing can also produce a relaxing effect.

Deep Breathing

Breathing should involve your entire torso, especially the abdominal wall muscles. Your ribs should expand in all directions, not just out to the front. Only by breathing naturally can you supply your brain with enough oxygen for concentration and your muscles with the oxygen they need to perform efficiently.

Fig. 66

Begin by emptying your lungs with a prolonged exhale in little puffs. Your hands should rest on your lower belly and should rise and fall with each breath. With practice this breathing will become natural, but at first you may encounter difficulty. Each inhale and each exhale should become longer and longer over the duration of this exercise. Begin by counting to three while breathing in, hold your breath for a moment and then breathe out while again counting to three. This rhythm can be increased to counts of 4, 5, etc. This breathing exercise can also be done while lying down or walking.

The benefits of this kind of breathing include centering and grounding, relaxation of the central nervous system, and creating rhythmic motions in the skull and jaw, thus releasing tension there as well.

Thumping the Thymus

In stressful situations people can also protect themselves against over-exertion by "knocking" (with their knuckles) on their sternums. The thymus' natural reflex is to "activate" itself and send out calming hormones. Everyone should do this at least once a day as protection from daily subconscious stress. People can calm themselves down in particularly stressful environments or situations by using this technique. The only animal that also uses this technique to calm itself in stressful situations is the ape, which pounds on its chest in exciting or precarious situations.

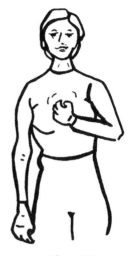

Fig. 66

Cobra

This exercise improves your ability to cross over the centerline of your body, as well as affecting your entire body posture, attention, breathing, and two-eyed 3D vision. Your back will relax as will your central nervous system, and your mind will become clearer.

Lie on your stomach on a firm mat. Push your upper body slowly up slightly off the ground, while, at the same time, slowly inhaling. Do NOT let your back arch (over-extend). Next, raise your head slowly and smoothly. This automatically extends your neck and chest. Keep your shoulders relaxed. Now let your body sink slowly back down onto the mat in this order; first, your chest, then your shoulders, your neck, and finally your head. While sinking back down exhale slowly, making sure that your esophagus is not compressed.

Fig. 67

Rider Warm-Up

All riders learn the importance of warming up their horses to avoid injury and to promote the best possible muscle development during the training part of the session, but many riders do not take the time to warm themselves up as well. This is especially important for the rider who only rides one time per week in a lesson, or who comes to the barn after sitting at a desk all day. Taking the time to do some basic warm-up exercises will help protect the rider against injury as well as giving her the best chance at being able to communicate effectively with her horse during the ride. A second purpose of a warm-up program is to become aware of and to learn how to lessen our individual muscular imbalances. All muscles have an ideal length, and we want to reclaim this ideal length as only then will the muscles work effectively.

Every rider has muscular imbalances that will cause problems/mistakes in riding. The rider and the trainer should be aware of where these come from and what general tendencies each rider has. It is also important to know which muscles and muscle groups are important for addressing these problems.

In daily life people use one side of their bodies more than the other, and often use their bodies incorrectly, or over-use them without properly preparing the muscles. Over-using the muscles results in a shortening and improper development of the muscle groups. An example of this is the body builder who concentrates on developing a very strong biceps muscle, but does not balance that with stretching and thus ends up not being able to straighten his arm completely. Shortened muscles can be improved (lengthened) through proper stretching exercises. Inactivity or too much stretching leads to weakening of muscle groups. Over–stretched muscles can be improved (shortened) through proper strengthening exercises. In both cases the goal is to use exercises to help the muscle obtain its ideal, balanced length.

Psychological stress adds to already physically unbalanced muscle groups, making correct use of them more difficult. Psychological conditions leave telltale marks in the body and can appear outwardly as physical difficulties. For example, when people are scared, their shoulders come up; when they feel dominated or oppressed, their body rhythms are disturbed. Aggressive temperaments may experience unfocused and uncontrolled energy outbursts. All these conditions may lead to making already unbalanced muscles even more unbalanced. (See *Exercise Program for Riders*, Meyners 2003 for an effective warm-up program).

INSTRUCTOR

Fundamentals of Teaching

In the previous sections we have discussed many important aspects of riding that are foundational to this practical section on the fundamentals of teaching. When instructors use these concepts, theories and exercises in their lessons they must also keep in mind which goals they and their pupils have and adapt each lesson to these goals. In a sense we have explored some of the "what" of teaching and now we turn to the "how" of teaching riding. Anybody who has experienced instruction from a variety of instructors knows that there are many different ways to convey information and to communicate between rider, instructor, and horse. This section will explore what makes some methods of instruction more often effective than others, and will help instructors and students to become better teachers and learners.

   Giving riding lessons is one of the most difficult teaching situations that exist. Instructors not only have one creature to deal with, but two! These two creatures function in entirely different ways from each other, which makes things even more complicated. The Rider Section illustrates some of the challenges students have when learning to ride and attempts to make these problems more understandable for instructors and students. The next step is to design lesson plans that organize these principles of learning and put them to use to deal with the difficulties that are often faced.

This chapter explains and gives examples of how this can (and should) be done.

Lesson planning is not an easy task, and too often instructors simply rely on older methods without expanding their horizons and using what really works. An instructor may have been taught under a certain method and thus believe that this is the only correct way to teach, or she may simply have become comfortable in whatever method seemed to "work" when she began teaching. While there may be some very beneficial parts to every instructor's teaching method, all instructors can benefit from examining their methods from time to time and trying new ways of communicating with rider and horse. While the essentials of "what" to teach have remained the same over many years, we now have a much better understanding of "how" people learn, so instead of projecting old and stagnant methods on new and individual people and horses, instructors need to be open to new and proven methods of instruction in order to obtain the very best results.

Problems can arise when any teaching method is projected onto all horses, because not all horses are the same. Each equine creature is very individual and unique—something typical teaching methods often do not take into account. Instructors must constantly adapt their teaching methods to fit the horses' and riders' specific personalities and needs. Due to the fact that not every instructor innately has the knowledge or ability to analyze a horse and rider correctly, pick the right lesson, and adapt it to the needs of their students, the process of selecting the right lesson for the moment is difficult for many instructors.

Instructors must also deal with the second creature in this mixture: the rider. The older methods of teaching horseback riding do not give instructors any hints or strategies for dealing with students and their unique personalities. When riding lessons are given to groups of people, dealing with riders' individual problems and needs becomes even more difficult. The older methods of instruction insist that students (riders) must act exactly like the books say and make the horse react exactly like the books say using a specific set of aids and motions that was assumed to work universally. However, as we have seen in the previous chapters, ideal people and ideal horses with ideal behaviors simply do not exist. We have seen how complicated learning actually is and that not every student (or every horse) learns in exactly the same way.

> *Problems can arise when any teaching method is projected onto all horses or all riders, because not all horses and riders are the same.*

In the process of writing this book I have assumed that riding instructors already have the qualifications necessary to teach horseback riding, including being educated themselves above the level of the students they are teaching. What instructors of all levels must learn, however, is how to organize their knowledge about riding into precise, methodical and effective lesson plans.

For quite some time now written lesson planning has been required of instructors in Germany. All German riding instructors must go through a series of courses followed by an exam in order to be certified to teach and train. Many instructors will reach their "B" and "A" level certifications, with fewer going on to achieve their "Pferdewirtschaftsmeister," which is like a Master's Degree in riding, training, and horse care. As part of their coursework students in each of these levels of certification learn to develop and use the written lesson plan. Writing out a lesson plan allows the instructor to organize their own knowledge about the Scale of Education for horses and riders, integrate it with their knowledge of the individual student and think about what methods might be the most effective for conveying a certain concept or feeling to a particular student. In group lessons this is even more important as the instructor may have students with very different learning styles and so may need to think about several ways of presenting the information that will help each student arrive at the correct feeling.

Keep in mind that this written lesson plan is only an outline; it still must be able to be modified based on circumstances or occurrences requiring special attention that arise during lessons. We all know and have experienced how quickly situations can change. This is due to the simple fact that there are two creatures learning the same things at the same time but in very different ways. An instructor's flexibility in situations where sudden direction changes in a lesson can occur reveals his or her qualities as a teacher. These changes should be anticipated in lesson planning as much as possible and flexibility must be built into the outline, as we will discuss later.

In addition to planning for each lesson, instructors and students need to develop a long term plan so that the overall picture and goals are clear. When this is done, students and instructors will be able to see how each individual riding lesson or practice ride fits into the big picture and helps bring a student closer to his or her goals. This kind of long-term planning is difficult, but it is important so that instructors and students are on the same page with their goals and the path they believe they are taking to get there. This makes these collective goals easier to visualize and attain.

Important Aspects of Lesson Planning

The lesson plan is the structure on which all of the components of effective instruction are put into action. The plan is what allows instructors' knowledge, methods, and teaching styles to be expressed.

Making Decisions

Instructors must be decision makers. Throughout the process of developing lesson plans, as well as during each actual lesson, instructors have many decisions to make, keeping in mind all of the various factors that influence each lesson. As we have already discussed, it is important for the student to play an active role in the learning process, so students need to be included in the decision making. At the very least, instructors must be sure that their lesson plans are understandable and logical so that students can follow the thought process of the instructor. The decisions that instructors make must also incorporate the individuality of each horse and rider.

TOPICS, GOALS AND CONTENTS OF RIDING LESSONS

What is the difference between a lesson topic, a lesson goal, and the lesson content? It is necessary to know what is actually behind these terms "topic," "goal," and "content," otherwise, the real essence of a lesson (or its structure) is unclear. At the beginning of lectures I like to ask the participants for their definitions of these terms. Although their answers vary, they do not really get to the core of these terms. People often define content as the topic or goal, and vice versa. While these terms are related, they are not the same thing.

Lesson planning theory in pedagogy has set concrete definitions for these terms, and instructors should be familiar with them in order to give effective lessons. Although definitions are not the sole purpose here, the substance of definitions gives instructors the necessary tools and criteria they need to build a good, effective lesson. The lesson **goal** is the big picture of what the instructor and student want to achieve during the lesson. The lesson **content** is a neutral activity that will be used to meet the goal. The lesson **topic** is the theme of the lesson and is made up of a goal paired with a specific content. Here are some examples of lesson topics with the goals and contents they are made up of:

- Jumping exercises (content) to improve submissiveness and obedience (goal)
- Transitions and curved lines (content) to improve coordination of aids (goal)
- Rhythmic and controlled (goal) jumping over natural barriers (content)
- Unmounted cross-coordination exercises (content) to improve rider's ability to ride a round circle (goal)

It should be clear to each instructor that all lesson topics can be changed to better-fit horse and rider when necessary. Instructors may have the same goal for two horses (i.e. improving submissiveness and obedience), but choose to use two different lesson contents to work towards that goal (i.e. jumping exercises or dressage exercises). When doing jumping exercises it is not only about just clearing the jump. These exercises must be constructed in such a way that the rider can use the jumps to help the horse become more submissive and obedient (see first example topic above). Once a clear lesson topic has been decided, the instructor can decide on the methods to be used in the lesson.

LEARNING GOALS

We just defined the lesson goal as the big picture describing what instructor and student want to achieve during a lesson. Learning goals are changes in the behavior of the horse or rider concerning the lesson topic. These changes include new motions that have not yet been learned. When developing learning goals, they must be formulated in such a way that they can be evaluated by an observer. This is usually done by listing criteria that must be met in order for the learning goal to be achieved.

The difference between a behavior and an action is this: "behavior" is a reaction, while "action" is a self-initiated activity. Because horses cannot think like humans they can only react. Riders cannot act independently when they must follow instructors' commands. Instead they react, thus behaving dependently. The learning goals used in the dialogue concept of teaching must enable riders to create a dialogue with the horse themselves, and thus should be focused on developing actions in the rider rather than just behaviors in response to the instructor's commands. The higher the rider's competence level is, the more independently he or she will be able to act.

Here are some examples of learning goals with evaluation criteria listed below each one. You will notice that the learning goal is listed as a "behavior/action." This is because it could be either one depending on how the instructor presents the task to the student. The instructor could use commands to get the student to perform the task (thus making the student's performance a behavior), or the instructor could use active learning methods to help the student achieve the task (thus making the student's performance an action).

- Riders should canter in a circle in a two-point (behavior/action) such that:
    – they can shorten and extend the canter stride (evaluation criterion),
    – they can canter over cavalletti on the circle without losing the rhythm (evaluation criterion),
    – they remain in harmony with the fluid motions of their horse (evaluation criterion).
- Riders should clear small jumps (behavior/action) such that:
    – they look at the jump in the right moment (evaluation criterion),
    – they use their outside aids in the turns (evaluation criterion),
    – their bodies follow the horse's body appropriately over the jump (evaluation criterion).

- Riders should approach the jumps (behavior/action) such that:
  - they choose the approach themselves (evaluation criterion),
  - their chosen approach is direct (evaluation criterion),
  - they find a rhythm with the horse (evaluation criterion).

TOOLS/ACCESSORIES

Having a plan for a lesson also allows instructors to know what tools or accessories they may need for a particular lesson topic. If the lesson topic is to longe the rider (content) in order to develop a deeper seat (goal), the instructor may bring a longe line, sidereins, and a longe whip. If the lesson topic is to use gridwork to help the horse develop proper striding before jumps the instructor will need to be sure that there are enough poles and standards to both create jumps and provide ground lines for the horse. Instructors can also make riding a circle or volte easier for beginner riders by putting out cones to mark where the circle line should be. These sorts of aids should be chosen ahead of time and put within reach so that the lesson does not have to be interrupted to fetch the needed material.

Lesson Requirements

The lesson requirements are all of the important elements that are necessary for effective instruction. They must be considered when the instructor is putting together the lesson plan as well as during the lesson itself. If certain aspects are left out, it will be very difficult to achieve effective teaching and learning.

Horse and Rider Demographics

Beyond the technical knowledge instructors must know as much as possible about their students, starting with the obvious and observable physical characteristics, and then also including the less easily determined (but just as important) psychological characteristics. When teaching individuals or groups, the instructor will need to make note of the students':

- age(s),
- current riding skills,
- learning and performance abilities,
- stamina of the group and individual members (condition/fitness abilities),
- skill level(s) of the horse(s).

The way the group is put together determines, for example, which topics and learning goals lessons can have. Lessons are based (and dependent) on the experience, abilities and skills that riders and horses bring with them, as well as their goals. Instructors cannot simply "plan" a lesson by just thinking up a topic. Instead, they must first carefully reflect on the horses and riders involved in order to plan a lesson. After analyzing these considerations instructors can then make choices about overall goals, content, and learning goals for their lessons.

Socio-Cultural and Educational Considerations

Instructors must also know about their riders' social and educational backgrounds. What kind of home environment, for example, do their young riders have? What is their relationship with their parents like? How do they do in school? Do they have any trouble or difficulties at school because of their ethnic origins or because of a learning disorder? The consideration of these social and learning ability aspects plays a serious role in the success or failure of lessons.

When working with adult riding students instructors should always consider which careers their students have chosen. Many adult riders transfer their "strategies for success" in their careers to their riding lessons, which may cause them to be too dominant with the horse and not patient enough with themselves. When riders have a leading position at work it is often difficult for them to take suggestions and tips from instructors.

Various life experiences can cause riders to be afraid of domineering teachers or adults. This can lead to aggression or aggressive behavior when an instructor acts very domineering or is gruff with his students instead of taking an advisory and guiding role.

Knowledge of Developmental Stages Regarding Coordination, Flexibility and Agility

Horseback riding instructors need to know about the abilities of the human body during the different developmental stages so that they do not overrate or underrate their students. If instructors are not educated in this area, they will be more likely to have difficulty interpreting the verbal and body language of their students correctly. Instructors must apply the following physical education criteria to be able to better assess their students' actions and better recognize their strengths and weaknesses.

INFANCY

While we are never in the position of educating infants in horseback riding, many of the developments that are supposed to occur during this developmental phase have an impact on children's, adolescents', and adults' abilities to learn during these later stages. In the first year of life a child develops basic coordination skills necessary for later advanced physical activities including specific gripping skills, upright posture skills and walking skills. Too often adults "help" an infant learn to walk by holding their hands in the air and helping them forward. Although these parents' intentions may be good, they are actually disrupting the natural development of the child.

Parents and adults must be aware that at this age sequenced motor skills begin to develop in the brain and slowly move their way throughout the body. The eyes determine how the head moves, which in turn determines how the hips and pelvis move. Coordination, or "cross-coordination," is essential for a child's further development. For example, a child must be able to lift her left arm and use her right leg at the same time while crawling. This "lizard-motion" is fundamental for large muscle coordination later, as well as for ensuring that all parts of the brain can communicate effectively with each other. Many children today skip the cross-coordination phase (developed when crawling) because they go straight from a sitting position to a walking position. As you can imagine, this causes coordination problems later on. It can also cause problems for using the correct "turning seat" in horseback riding. A rider with this kind of difficulty is not able to hold his hips parallel to the horse's hips at the same time that he holds his shoulders parallel to the horse's shoulders since this requires cross-coordination ability. Instead this rider will try to turn "like a bus" holding his shoulders and hips parallel to each other rather than to the body parts of the horse. The effect of this crooked seat is that the rider can never steer the horse correctly.

Basic motor skills are developed between 2 and 3 years of age. Children learn basic actions, such as walking, climbing up and down, running, jumping, balancing, etc. However, almost all development takes place in the large muscles. (Further development of the large muscles is described in the following sections). At this stage children learn by copying others. Toddlers' spatial orientation, adaptation, discernment and balancing abilities are only slightly developed. At this stage children are very curious, interested in trying everything out and discovering their environment. This is why children need ample space to jump, run, play, scream, climb, etc. without restraint.

EARLY CHILDHOOD (4–7 Years)

At this age children learn to combine actions and motions. Due to constant physical play, where they like to test their physical abilities, they can usually balance fairly well. Children unconsciously improve their balancing abilities while playing. Children at this age also start to learn rhythm. Balance is rhythm and rhythm is balance! We call it "gracefulness." So, while they are balanced, they are also rhythmical! Acoustic stimuli, such as music, can be easily converted to different rhythms, such as hopping, running and galloping. It is important that range of motion is well developed in all the large joints (ankle, knee, hip and shoulder) for good agility. However, specialized training is not necessary.

MIDDLE CHILDHOOD (7–10 Years)

In this stage, children who were very active as toddlers quickly develop additional motor skills. During middle childhood the development of motor skills is essentially complete. Children who are very active usually have the best motor skills. During this stage the growth rate is more intense than during any other time. Gender differences are still irrelevant; so the same can be expected of both boys and girls. Coordination abilities are easily learned, however agility is not so evident at this age. Although 7 to 9 or 10–year–old children usually have good general agility, they have trouble spreading their legs far apart and turning their shoulders outwards. At the same time, however, the flexibility in their hips, shoulder joints, and back increases. Even at this age it may be beneficial to do a little stretching to improve the elasticity of those muscles prone to shorten (hamstrings, hip flexors and pectorals) to reduce the chance of shortening in adulthood (see Meyners 2003/2).

LATE CHILDHOOD
(10–12 Years for Girls/10–13 Years for Boys)

There is actually less development in this stage than in both of the earlier stages. The yearly growth rate usually levels off at around age 11 for girls and about 13 for boys. Children at this age are usually able to understand and perform instructed actions and movements successfully. They learn easily and can immediately convert given instruction into reality. Of course, early development of coordination and fitness abilities determines how coordinated a child is at this age. Regarding horseback riding, children should be schooled in the basics: balance, rhythm and differentiating between certain muscles. They should also have lessons in basic jumping and dressage, and gain experience with different ponies or horses. Only when children are allowed to "let go" and really get into something can they learn and experience balance and rhythm, which are crucial for learning to "feel" (becoming one with the horse) later.

The level of agility at this age is fairly similar to that of the previous stage. However, flexibility of the spine, hips and shoulders is more evident at this age, and 10 to 13-year-olds are more capable of specific activities. Nevertheless, there is a danger that muscle groups begin to become misbalanced at this age. Therefore, it is very important to cross train the weaker muscles and keep an upright posture. Otherwise young riders will not be able to ride smoothly or with balance. (See Meyners 2003/2.)

PRE- AND EARLY TEENS / PUBERTY
(12–14 Years for Girls/13–15 Years for Boys)

In this stage of childhood, coordination development stagnates or at least slows down for a while, earlier for girls than for boys. Researchers have found that learning new motor skills is more difficult during puberty than in childhood. Instructors and trainers cannot expect too much from pre-teens and young teens. They must also be prepared for minimal performances from riders at this age. These lanky, chunky or otherwise clumsy kids are going through growth spurts that cause their legs to suddenly be longer than normal and their muscles to do odd things. At the same time they have to deal with large amounts of hormones in their blood streams. Their bodies and motor skills are undergoing large-scale renovations, also known as agility development.

While shoulder joints and inside thigh muscles have a tendency to become more inflexible, the upper body muscles (for bending forward) and the outer thigh muscles (for spreading the legs) increasingly become more flexible. Generally, girls are more flexible than boys. However, both girls' and boys' flexibility depend on the amount of exercise and stretching that they do.

LATE TEENS (14–17 Years for Girls / 15–19 Years for Boys)

Teens are able to be more dynamic in their actions and can better perform goal-oriented tasks. Although boys are especially coordinated at this age, both genders can use physical prowess to improve their learning abilities. Teens have a strong desire to strive for and accomplish goals, which helps them learn quickly. If teens (especially boys) train intensely and effectively they can be quite successful at their chosen sport. The same is true for girls who train at a high athletic level. Teenage girls are capable of learning quite complicated motor skills. However, if they do not engage in intense physical activity at this age, their coordination abilities can begin to deteriorate.

The development of flexibility in the large joints during the teen years is not the same for both genders. In general, girls are more flexible than boys. Until around the age of 20 specific muscle groups can be trained for optimal flexibility and agility. However, if certain muscle groups have not been used intensely by the age of 10, these muscles will never be very flexible. Inactivity will cause muscle imbalances rather quickly in both genders.

EARLY ADULTHOOD (18–35 Years)

Motor skill development is completed during adult life in day-to-day actions and work tasks. Men tend to perform actions efficiently and purposely. Work-related motions are exact, steady and sure. This precision comes from an automation of activity (muscle memory).

Similar tendencies are evident in women, too. Their motor functions increasingly show efficiency and rationality of purpose. On the whole, women's motor skills seem to be gender-specific. Their actions are softer, rounder, freer and more relaxed. Since women are not as muscular as men, their actions are more flexible—evident in the way they walk, for example. This flexibility in actions also helps explain why women are more spontaneous in their physical expressions.

In general, the level of habituation (automation) and the ability of expressive body language reveal the physical maturity level of an individual. After 20 to 30 years physical development plateaus and remains steady. The athletic accomplishments a person makes during this decade can never be topped. This period in life is known as the physical ability "peak." This is true especially for men, who achieve their coordination peak the earliest, and, according to studies, lose these physical abilities earlier than women.

However, not all men or women have the same physical abilities. Individual ability is greatly influenced by personal fitness and health. We will not discuss general fitness further since it is not extremely relevant for horseback riding.

MIDDLE AGE ADULTHOOD (30–50 Years)

At this age motor skills begin to fade; the level of achievement is noticeably lower. This stage of life can be labeled the "decade of gradual decline in motor skills." Although day-to-day motor functions stay at approximately the same level, physical motor skills dwindle, especially for those individuals who are generally unskilled.

The deficiency in ability to learn new skills is in part due to a decrease in coordination ability and general fitness. The realization that coordination and fitness abilities have declined and made an impact on the level of accomplishment tends to lead to a self-esteem crisis (also known as the "middle age crisis"). Nonetheless, I would like to point out that it is still possible to learn new skills, such as horseback riding. You can teach an old dog new tricks! Recent research has refuted the old belief that intelligence declines after age 40 or 50. The brain is still creating new cells and connections, which can be used to learn new skills and knowledge; so it is not hopeless! There are many effective "exercise" programs for body and mind available to help middle age and older adults remain healthy, active, and fit; and to prevent decline.

LATE ADULTHOOD (45–70 Years)

Motor skill functions deteriorate the most at this stage. It is unfortunately an irreversible process. Even in day-to-day activities and tasks at work the transformation is evident; learning to use new equipment is difficult, and any adaptation to progress is more difficult than it was years ago. Differences in individual abilities that were not apparent in earlier years are now considerable. Some 50 or 60-year-olds seem to lose their abilities fairly early, while others are still very resilient and peppy. The decreases in coordination abilities and flexibility make learning new behavior very challenging indeed, although not impossible! Weight gain impedes day-to-day activities, as well as physical activities. Those adults who remain active in body and mind experience the least decline in these areas, and remain healthy and able to learn and perform as long as they choose.

Content Analysis of Riding Lessons

Instructors must always have the lesson's structure in their head. They must be aware of the complexities involved in lesson content and goals and which motion requirements are called for in certain topics. Most instructors ride on a much higher level than their students. They have already learned the skills that they are teaching their students and do not even have to think about how to perform them; they just do it. It is exactly this vast difference between instructor and rider that can lead to communication problems because instructors have a difficult time putting themselves in their students' shoes and understanding their struggles. Aspects of skills that riders may not even be conscious of are the same things that instructors take for granted.

Instructors must make a detailed analysis of each skill they wish to impart. They must be aware of which aids a skill requires as well as the appropriate timing for those aids. Only then can they decide on a method to help the student learn that particular skill. This order in lesson planning is important because certain aids are the mechanical requirements that are absolutely necessary for the skill to be performed, while other aids are used for more fine tuning of the skill and can be left out at first. Once the rider has mastered the basics, the additional aids can be introduced. If instructors try to teach students the aids all at once their students would become frustrated and overwhelmed, both emotionally and mentally, and they would not be able to perform the skill at all.

The process of analyzing the content of lessons is detailed and takes a lot of time, but it is well worth the effort. Only through understanding the content at such a detailed level can instructors truly be effective in their teaching. In my experience at numerous conferences, I have seen that too many instructors unfortunately underestimate the content analysis of lessons.

Didactical Reasoning in Lessons

It is not enough for instructors to simply have a lesson goal and lesson contents and to analyze the contents. Instructors must also be able to explain to the student why they did all of this. Why is this particular goal important for this horse and rider and why did the instructor choose this particular lesson content to use to work towards the goal? How did they analyze the content and come up with these particular steps and criteria for evaluation? In this part of lesson planning instructors must demonstrate the relevance of the lesson topic for horseback riding and why they have chosen a particular lesson content for a specific rider and a specific horse. After analyzing the content instructors can begin to state their reasoning. They must include which aspects they chose for which horse and which rider. In this phase content analysis and horse/rider demographics are intertwined.

Methods in the Dialogue Concept of Horseback Riding

After instructors have chosen the topic, goals, and content for a lesson, analyzed the content and demonstrated its relevance, they can then decide how they will organize the lesson and which teaching methods they will use (see Principles of Effective Teaching and Riding, page 11). Instructors can make decisions about whether their lesson will be direct or indirect. It is important that instructors consider how a lesson should be organized. They need to decide whether they are working toward goals for individual riders or for the entire group. The organizational structure of a lesson must be determined before the lesson begins and should be explained to the riders. As a rule, instructors should discuss lessons with their students one-on-one to make sure they are both "on the same page."

METHODS IN A HOLISTIC APPROACH

If horseback riding is seen as a dialogue between horse and rider (see Rider Section page 31), then commands cannot be the central aspect of riding lessons. Instead, lessons should be about gathering basic experience in horseback riding exercises and drills. Choosing a basic approach to riding can simplify the ways of solving different riding challenges, including the ability to balance in various gaits and while turning (for example, in circles), the ability to be and stay in the rhythm of the horse's motion, and having a supple seat while going over jumps. Of course, an effective rider should also be able to handle a multitude of possible situations that may arise during the course of a ride.

Instruction and doing exercises are two different things. With the help of instruction students can determine exactly how to complete a certain motion. An exercise is more of an open-ended lesson because it allows the rider to develop various solutions on his own. It can also be called a "task," which the rider is given and for which he has to figure out a solution. Before and during an exercise or task instructors and students must discuss the criteria for a particular motion. This is important because an incorrect motion should not be practiced. It is also very important that the situation does not become dangerous and that the horse does not become confused by any vague motions or aids by the student.

Three methods for holistic instruction can be developed in accordance with the basic concepts of Gordijn when horseback riding is seen as a dialogue (see Tamboer 1979. Trebels 1990, 1992, 1993). Gordijn speaks of 1) direct dialogues, 2) learned dialogues, and 3) reaching one's limit. This last term simply refers to a rider reaching and then going beyond his physical limit while dealing with his "environment" (in this case his horse). I have reformulated these methods and his terminology for this book and will discuss methods for 1) direct learning, 2) achieving goals, and 3) creativity and inventiveness in lessons. These three methods are usually woven together in each lesson taught by an instructor following the holistic approach. The instructor must experiment to discover what the appropriate mix of all three is for each individual student.

Methods for Direct Learning
This approach describes the spontaneous behavior a child, young adult or adult has with a horse. In the farming tradition, for example, chil-

dren have the chance to develop playful relationships with the ponies on a horse farm. From a "country" perspective this relationship between pony and child is totally normal; they do not learn in an indoor arena from an instructor who shouts commands at them, but rather they "domesticate" the horse in an open field or in its stall.

In contrast to earlier times, this type of relationship between horse and human is not so easy to attain in today's world. However, it can be accomplished with an instructor who gives lessons on basic experience and behavior with the horse. Horseback riding techniques can then slowly develop out of this kind of learning situation, enabling the student to really understand the techniques and become more aware of them while riding. Early experience with a pony can be transferred later to a bigger horse.

This type of method is not necessarily applicable to only children or youth; it is also just as good for adults who happen to learn horseback riding later in life. Adults, in particular, should adapt to such methods because otherwise they will ride too "logically" and not become accustomed to the different motions and feelings of the horse. Use of a saddle should be avoided at this stage because the rider gets much more out of the dialogue principle (interaction between a rider's seat and the horse's back) if he or she is in direct contact with the horse.

The goal here is to have feeling of motion at the center of riding lessons. In the beginning stages it is very important that students learn basic holistic interactions (how the horse moves, how a rider must adapt to the horse or how the horse reacts if a rider makes certain motions). They must feel what influence they have on the horse when they sit left or right, forward or backward, etc. Students must also experience how a horse has to move in order to stay balanced and maintain its rhythm. This method allows students to become acquainted with a wide range of motions that will enable them to learn more advanced horseback riding techniques with ease. Complicated lessons are not effective at this point.

Methods for Achieving Goals
Striving for a particular goal focuses the student's activities on a particular purpose. Students must, however, find the path to this goal

on their own (of course, with their instructor's guidance). Rider and instructor work together to determine a learning goal as well as discussing the basic skills necessary for completing that learning goal. The instructor may also discuss with the student what criteria could be used to evaluate the learning goal. Then the rider has a chance to try to achieve the goal based on her own thoughts and ideas about how it might work. The instructor's role is to give feedback through the use of comments and questions after the rider has completed her first attempt. In order for students to be able to attain the learning goals they set themselves, they need to learn to see the lesson in a holistic way (the "big picture"). The following example may help illustrate this idea.

Riding a Circle: The instructor and student decide on a learning goal of riding a circle such that the horse stays on the intended path, the circle is round, and the rider uses his twisting seat appropriately. The student must find his own personal solution to the situation at hand, meaning that the student must figure out how to use his body to get the horse to travel on the intended route. The instructor determines the intended path for the horse by either setting out cones or drawing a line in the dirt. Instructors can also ride the circle first as an example or show a video of someone riding a circle. The most important motions needed are discussed with the student in detail, such as positioning of the hips and shoulders, and then the student is asked what thoughts or ideas he has for riding the circle and fulfilling the evaluative criteria. After this discussion the practical component can begin; in this example, the instructor sends the student out to try to ride a circle while meeting the agreed upon evaluative criteria.

After a student has attempted to reach the learning goal the instructor can discuss further strategies with the student. The instructor can ask the student whether he thought he achieved his learning goal. Did the horse stay on the intended route? Was the circle round? Did he use his twisting seat appropriately? Based on the outcome of the first attempt new criteria can be discussed for performing the task, and the student can try again, integrating his experience of the first attempt into this next attempt. The experience is always approached from a holistic perspective, examining the motions of horse and rider and how they interact. The student must feel (experience) how his own motions influence the horse's motions and vice versa. Riders must act according to the motions of the horse in every situation. This method of feeling the horse's reactions and changing one's own reactions accordingly should be followed until the student can solve the given situation correctly using the right techniques.

Methods for Creativity and Inventiveness

Creativity and inventiveness are only possible when students have mastered the basic motions required for the lesson. Only after both horse and rider are fully in harmony can the rider become creative and inventive with his motions. More challenging goals can be continuously developed after the rider has become skilled in one area and is able to work together well with his horse. At this stage students can develop more advanced solutions and various combinations of strategies on their own to achieve the learning goals. Going back to our example, once the rider has a solid feel or muscle memory for what the correct circle is, then he can experiment with a variety of aids and methods to see if he can achieve the same result using different or perhaps more subtle aids and communication. The rider can also use creativity to change the size of the circle or the location of the circle in the arena. He may decide to experiment with spiraling the horse in and out on a circle, or riding a figure eight. All of these variations are only possible once the initial learning goal has been met and the aids committed to muscle memory.

Observation and Mental Training

Simply watching horseback riding facilitates a certain understanding of motion processes. This can be useful in internalizing and learning the observed motion. Mental training is based on systematic repetition of inner thought processes and feeling motion. In other words, riders should concentrate on a specific motion in their imagination and let this motion play out inside their heads before they actually perform it. It is through a similar process that instructors "ride with" their students, feeling in their own bodies what they are observing in their students.

Observation training produces a visual picture of motion inside a rider's brain. This visual picture guides her motions later and influences how she performs. The more that a rider is able to observe a motion being performed correctly, the more clear her inner, visual picture of that motion becomes. By watching complicated motions the rider will also gain a better understanding of and ability to perform basic motions. The ability to imagine a specific motion is the visual aspect that accompanies the development of motor skills. Riders can further develop their motor skills and enhance their "feel" for riding by mentally practicing riding motions.

It is best to start mental training when a rider has developed some basic competencies and has experienced feel. When a rider visualizes a specific motion his body undergoes certain biological and chemical changes that would also take place if he were actually performing the motion. Therefore, it is logical that if a rider visualizes a specific action before carrying it out, he will have much better results than if he were to perform it without being mentally prepared.

The goal of observation is to improve a rider's performance by enhancing his perception and visualization abilities. Through intensive application of self-observation and mental preparation students can improve their coordination (the entire interaction of the muscular system). The systematic activities of the human brain must be turned into processes based on feeling (see Rider Section–How Riders Learn—Active Learning, page 18), where the rider's feelings unite with those of the horse. This transition from systematic, thinking activities to physical and emotional feeling and perception is very important for learning how to have a dialogue with a horse.

How Observation Helps Us to Feel

One important goal of horseback riding instruction is to motivate students to be consistently in harmony with their horses under many conditions. Riders should independently test their abilities and their horse's abilities by riding under various conditions, such as in an indoor ring, in an outdoor ring, in the forest, etc.). It is only possible to teach students to be independent when each individual participant in a lesson is respected and their needs and abilities are carefully considered. Once students have learned to work on their own they can then begin to learn to feel their own body and to feel the horse by regularly employing observation and mental training in their training routines.

This kind of teaching helps students learn to have goals and intentions. Riding instructors should base their lessons on reinforcing their riders' abilities (not focusing on what they have not yet mastered) and then make every effort to create lessons with a wide variety of motions. Instructors can make the intentions and goals of certain riding motions understandable to their students by explaining the criteria for a motion, performing the motion or showing a series of pictures or a short video of the motion. Visual aids, as well as recalling earlier riding experiences, can help students learn a specific riding motion.

It is important that riders are not overwhelmed with learning a motion; in order to stay motivated they must always believe that they are able to master the motion. Learning new motions is very closely linked to earlier experiences. For students to be motivated enough to want to learn more instructors must assure them that they are capable of performing a motion correctly. Instructors must assure their students of their own abilities and provide assistance when needed. This is important for instructors to remember because even the best riding students do not get everything right the first time.

Supporting Riders' Appreciation for Holistic Connections

Instructors can help their students understand motions in their entirety and the purposes behind each component by discussing the criteria for that motion with them. It is not enough for the student to be able to perform well if instructors simply demonstrate the motion for them. Verbal communication is what makes it possible for a student to understand each motion and each component of that motion and, therefore, the motion as a whole. This understanding allows the student to develop the appropriate feel for the motion and the ability to reproduce the motion on her own.

To create a specific reaction in the horse a rider must give him a cue or make a specific motion (or intention) himself. Weight and leg aids are more important than any other aids when cantering, for example, because without them the horse would not cooperate.

Instructors and riders must clarify the application of these important aids beforehand. Instructors must also create a good environment where the motion is likely to occur, so that the student has the best opportunity to experience the motion and begin developing the accompanying feel. Instructors and students can work on other, more subtle aids after these "trigger aids" have been well mastered.

Instructors Must Teach Students to Feel

By teaching students to feel instructors enhance the development of their riders' inner dialogues. Instructors can use self-observation exercises so that students learn to see themselves "from the inside." Instead of correcting students directly after their performances, instructors should ask which aids the student used and which ones the horse reacted to. Even if a student has not yet fully grasped a motion, he should still try to describe the aids that he used and the motion that he felt. By comparing students' descriptions and actual performances, instructors can recognize how well their students observed their own motions and those of their horse and whether they actually felt the motion or just assumed that it was happening.

Students should be encouraged to self-correct (this is an inner dialogue, or self-talk) from the beginning, and instructors should take more of an advisory or coaching roll. The use of media (especially videos of students' own performances) can be very helpful with appropriate guidance so that students do not focus only on the negative, but instead learn to see the things they are doing correctly as well as the places where they need further development.

Constant interaction between riding, assessing feeling, analyzing, making new goals and discussing motions with the instructor helps students' performances become more exact. Their motions become engrained and imprinted in their brains through feeling rather than thought. Students are able to increasingly catch their own mistakes and deviations and describe them, find the causes and eventually, with help from their instructor, correct them. They no longer have to "think" about performing a motion because their brain has transferred the knowledge to their senses. The brain simply gives the cue and it "happens." Instructors not only get an overview of their students' ability to explain, to question, to correct, to describe and to perform, but also an overview of their abilities to absorb, understand and store information.

Methods to Improve the Development of "Feel"

Throughout the lesson the instructor is doing everything possible to support the student's effort to improve the development of their feel. To this end, the instructor's methods are very important. This includes the words and phrases they use, their ability to help the student focus inwardly and the tools they use to create a situation that best allows the student to feel. (More on this in Teaching Styles in the Arena, page 177.)

Instructors Should Not Overwhelm Their Students with Requirements

Riding a circle or a volte is not an easy exercise for any rider, even if the instructor tells him or her exactly what to do. If the instructor simply stands in the center of the intended circle, it becomes a much easier task. Riders' actions become automatic if they have to look at their instructor in the center of the circle. Commands are unnecessary in this situation. Eye contact replaces the use of many words and makes it easier for riders to perform the correct motions. When students hold eye contact with the instructor their outer shoulder is slightly turned forward, the outer rein is looser, the inner rein is slightly shortened, the horse will be in the right position, and the student sits very well in the saddle. Students also have an easier time turning the horse and keeping it aligned on the intended circle line.

In general, instructors should consider what visual aids they can employ in their lessons to make learning easier for their students without overwhelming them with numerous rules. In the circle example above, if the instructor tried to explain all of the various aids to the student to get the horse onto a round circle, the student may have felt overwhelmed and the circle would not have happened so smoothly. By using a simple visual aid the instructor was able to reduce the requirements he had to tell the student, and yet the student was able to perform the necessary motions to ride a correct circle, thus allowing the student to begin to develop the proper feeling of being on a circle. Another example can be seen in the show jumping arena. How often do show jumping horses land on the wrong lead after clearing a fence? In this situation instructors often emphasize that the student should press down in one stirrup or another to counterbalance the horse. This usually does not solve the problem since it requires too much thought and perfect timing. If instructors teach their students to simply concentrate on the remaining jumps and focus on the next jump while in the air the horse usually lands on the correct lead. A person's gaze determines their movement (Feldenkrais).

The use of cones as a visual aid in riding a zigzag line, for example, allows action commands to be reduced. Simply the visual stimulus of the cones makes the situation easier to master. Students can recognize their own deviations better and, with some assistance from their instructor, perform the correct motions more rapidly. Keeping commands to a minimum allows the maximum opportunity for the student to focus on the feeling.

Opposing Motions are Important in Order to Better Understand Actual Motions

Having the rider intentionally sit "incorrectly" can help the rider develop the feeling for the "correct" way of sitting. Using opposing motions, or motions which are different from the intended motion, ironically gives riders more security in knowing where the intended motions should be. All motions should be performed intentionally slowly and quickly, large and small, firmly and gently so that riders become sensitive to the more subtle variations. The different reactions of the horse to each of these kinds of motions are particularly important for finding out what effect certain motions have on a horse.

Students can get a feel for the "correct" seat by sitting too far to the right, then too far to the left, then leaning too far forward and leaning too far backward. Their brain is confronted with various possible sitting positions in the saddle, none of which feels right. After trying out these extreme positions riders should then sit in the saddle normally again. They will be able to simply feel the "correct" seat because their brain will choose the correct position out of all the options that were presented to it. This is much more effective than having the instructor mold the student into a "correct" position and tell them to stay there. In this case the rider has not learned how to get into that position from the extremes, and will end up very stiff and tense trying to remain "correct" and perhaps being fearful of what will happen if she moves from that position. If the rider discovers her own "correct" seat through experimentation, she will be very comfortable there, and it will be easy for her to make subtle adjustments as needed to remain balanced and centered over the horse without tension and without concentration.

Pictures Instead of Commands

Giving students pictures and images (metaphors) to work with rather than commands is extremely helpful in learning. The use of imagery and metaphors reduces any misinterpretations and unwanted variations of meaning. Here are some commands that could be interpreted very differently by different students:

"Hold the reins gently."

"Sit up straight!"

The words "gently" and "straight" can have very different meanings for different people. If, however, the instructor uses metaphors, he is much more likely to get the intended result. So he may say:

"Hold the reins as if you were holding a baby bird in your hand."

"Sit proudly!"

"Make yourself as tall as a giant!"

Unless they don't like birds, most people will have a similar amount of firmness in their hands when imagining holding a baby bird. While there still may be some differences, it is much more defined than the word, "gently." The same is true with the word "straight." When told to sit "straight" many riders end up stiff, but when told to sit "proudly" they will bring their bodies into a position of straightness that is appropriate for them. Using the word "tall" in association with a giant gives riders an image to put in their mind as they figure out what to do with their own individual bodies to make them similar to a giant's body.

Instructors have to choose images relevant to the particular riding situation and each individual student. The correct use of imagery can improve a student's feeling for motion.

Focusing a Student's Attention Internally

When students learn motion they are also learning to perceive. Students' attention should be focused on the quality of their motion. Focusing students' attention internally means that instructors should give their students tasks (according to their skill level) in which students must pay special attention to how they complete an action. It is important in using opposing motions in particular, that students learn to feel changes in their horse resulting from the changes they make within their own body.

Specific skills can be divided up into smaller elements so that the student can specifically work on the dynamic sequence of a motion. In this type of lesson instructors have a wide range of choices as to how they ask their students to describe their observations. For example, they can ask for an overall description of the student's inner feeling or a detailed step-by-step description of how the feeling changed over the course of the motion sequence.

Planning the Course of a Lesson
THE WRITTEN LESSON PLAN

This is where we put the various theories, methods, styles and techniques into action. Once we know the background of the students we must make a decision of what we want to teach. We make a plan, considering the learning goals for each student, but being certain to remain flexible when we enter the arena. The written lesson plan is the structure on which all of the components of effective instruction are put into action. The plan allows instructors' knowledge, methods, and teaching styles to be expressed. Our planning continues by organizing the topic, goal and content and then putting them into effect with the basic structure of the lesson itself.

Diagram 5

LESSON TOPIC: LEARNING GOAL:				
Time	Skill/Exercise	Organization	Focus/Learning Goal	Possible Deviation/Solution

Instructors must have a general idea of how long each phase of a lesson will take, although strictly adhering to the allotted time is not imperative. These times should only be general estimations in service of an organized structure. Each exercise to be used towards achieving the goal should be written down and briefly described. Next, the order of exercises should be noted as well as whether it is for all riders or only some of the group, if it is a group lesson. Each exercise should work toward a specific focus or learning goal, which should be precisely articulated. The last column is labeled "possible deviations and solutions." Instructors should consider which deviations students could make and which alternatives could help bring the student(s) forward. The more flexible instructors are the easier

LEARNING GOAL:	NAME:		
LESSON CONTENT:			
Nr.	Exercise	Focus	Possible Deviations
1.			
2.			
3.			
4.			
5.			
6.			
7.			
8.			
9.			
10.			
Tools / Accessories			
Organization form			
Video			
Training and exercise suggestions for independent work:			
Hints or suggestions for next lesson:			

Diagram 6

it is to articulate these goals. In other words, when the instructor realizes that this is a guideline, not something set in stone, it is easier to write out this plan.

In contrast to Diagram 5, the lesson plan in Diagram 6 includes suggestions for independent work and references for the following lesson. These additions show the rider what exercises he or she can expect in the coming lessons and also what long-term goals and ideas the instructor has in mind. Letting students know what to expect and what long-term goals and perspectives their instructor has in mind for them motivates and encourages them to work together towards these goals. Participating and working with their instructor on exercises and lessons is the basis for effective change, both short- and long-term, for students. (*see Appendix for samples of Diagrams 5 & 6*)

Basic Lesson Structure

Having a structured routine within the lesson itself frees the student to focus on the important information the instructor is teaching rather than wondering what is coming next. The benefits of a predictable sequence for teaching include not only more relaxed students (who know in general what to expect and what will be expected of them), but also a more relaxed instructor (who knows in general what to do and when). Students often will take the structure of the lesson home to their practice sessions, making these sessions more productive. Although there are variations, basic lesson structure, whether for an individual or group, includes several parts:

Greeting: The purpose of the greeting is to bring instructors and students into the present moment, catching up on news, and letting go of anything extraneous that might get in the way of the lesson. For new students, instructors can use this time to put the students at ease as well as discussing what the student can expect and finding out what the student's hopes for the lesson are. In all cases, instructors are making a quick assessment of horse and rider inside and out.

Warm-up: The purpose of the warm-up is to give the instructor a chance to watch the students as they prepare for their lesson without offering assistance. This period of observation gives instructors a general idea of the level of the student's riding as well as the rider's state of mind. With a returning student, the instructor will be able to see whether the horse and rider have improved since the last lesson, whether they confirmed any muscle memories or "feels" learned during the previous session, or whether perhaps a review is needed. This is the time for the instructor to review his or her lesson plan in light of the reality of what the horse and rider look like this day. When teaching a beginner, this phase will be guided by the instructor.

Warm-up review: The warm-up review is one of the most important discussions during the lesson. This review allows both rider and instructor a chance to "get on the same page" about their lesson goals as well as the content, based on how the horse and rider feel during the ride so far.

Main body of the lesson: The purpose of this part of the lesson is to work towards a learning goal using a mixture of the methods of direct learning, achieving goals, and creativity, as is appropriate. This part of the lesson will probably involve several "sets" where each set is made up of an initial theory discussion and plan followed by the rider's attempt to perform the desired motion followed by a review of what worked well and what still needs to be improved. This will then lead into the theoretical discussion for the next attempt by the rider to achieve the learning goal. If the rider is able to meet the goal for the lesson, the main body of the lesson should finish with some quiet time where the instructor allows the student a few minutes to practice her newly discovered feel to be sure that it is fixed in muscle memory and ready to be repeated at home before the next lesson.

Lesson review: The purpose of the lesson review is to bring even deeper awareness and further clarity to what was learned during the lesson and to plan the practice between lessons. The instructor can ask the student questions to ascertain the student's level of understanding about what they learned that day, and the student can ask the instructor any questions that they may have as a result of experiencing a new feeling. Then the student and instructor can discuss how the student should proceed between lessons to most effectively continue progress toward the long-term goals.

What Instructors Need to Know
QUALIFICATIONS

Riding instructors need to have sound technical skills, a thorough understanding of developmental stages and psychology, as well as highly tuned assessment skills so they know 'what' to teach.

Sound Technical Skills
As has been mentioned earlier in this book, we are assuming that instructors have the proper technical skills and personal background in riding to be able to assist horses and riders to learn. I recognize that this is not always the case, and sometimes people do become "instructors" without the proper technical training, but addressing this problem is not the goal of this book. Suffice it to say that instructors must take the time and make the effort to become well-educated and must have the attitude of a lifelong learner prior to beginning to instruct other horses and riders. In a similar manner to how important it is for a beginner rider to ride an educated horse, a beginner rider needs a very well-educated instructor so that they learn the basics correctly. It is much harder to go back and make corrections once a foundation has been laid.

It is important for instructors to have skills above the level of the student they are teaching so that they can hold the larger picture in their minds and help the student see the path he is following, including what will be coming up in the future. It is also essential that instructors continue their own education in teaching and riding skills.

Teaching Styles in the Arena

As we all know, teaching styles have a considerable influence on how we learn. The different styles of teaching horseback riding can either hinder or encourage learning. Riders often have a misconception that they will only be able to learn if they are being yelled at by their instructor. I have had students say to me, "Don't be nice! Yell when I do something wrong." I believe that this response stems from students' real desire to learn and improve, and their mistaken thought that they must be criticized in order for this to happen. Once riders understand that being yelled at does not mean that they will learn more (and actually it can mean the opposite!), riders usually prefer a rather easy-going style to a commanding, very controlling style. Constant commands tend to create stress for the rider, thus obstructing effective learning. Naturally, there are also those students who have grown accustomed to their instructor's gruff tone and seem to work well with this style of instruction. These different interpretations of an instructor's tone and style point to the fact that each student is different and should be taught appropriately. In other words, instructors need to get to know their students and try to create a personalized learning environment.

Communication Skills

In this section I will discuss how instructors can have either a strengthening or a weakening effect on their students. Bear in mind, I have not forgotten the ability of the riders to positively influence their own learning environment and, therefore, improve their riding skills.

WORDS
- Words, while not the only important form of communication, are certainly important. Instructors need to try to put comments in their positive form as often as possible.
- The type of words used is also important. "Feeling" words are very valuable, especially when the student is able to identify their own "feeling" words.

TONE OF VOICE
- Instructors' voices can have a therapeutic effect on their students. The overall intonation produces positive (or negative) vibrations, depending on the student. Not all students learn best with the same intonation from their instructor. Therefore, it is very important that each student feels comfortable enough to express his or her individual needs, and instructors should carefully watch their students' responses to their tone of voice and ask the student how they are feeling during the lesson. This way the communication between instructors and students is based on harmony and trust.

GESTURES AND EMOTIONS
- Instructors' gestures and facial expressions have a powerful effect on their students.
- Emotions (moods) also have a very strong effect. Therefore, it is important that instructors learn to control their emotions and turn pessimistic moods into optimistic moods. Students (and horses!) can usually tell when an instructor has had a bad day, and they may be reluctant to ask questions or interact with the instructor in that situation, thus impeding their learning abilities. It is the instructor's responsibility to put the students at ease, perhaps by admitting the bad mood but promising not to let it affect interactions with the student. The saying "our chemistry is off" has a lot of truth in it. By putting your face into the shape of a smile, you will release chemicals in your body that actually make you feel happier! A smile or a pleasant expression can significantly improve the atmosphere or general mood. Smiling uses chains of muscles that facilitate energy flow, while a grimace or a frown cuts this flow off.
- Nodding and shaking one's head have various meanings and functions for individuals as well as culturally. Signals and gestures of agreement or disagreement influence the flow of energy regulated by the thymus gland. For example, observers' gestures or body language have either a negative or positive effect on riders. If a rider sees his instructor shaking her head out of the corner of his eye his body will automatically block. His psychological energy diminishes. Whereas, on the other hand, if the instructor nods her head she gives the rider confidence and support for his actions. This applies to other observers as well; their head movements and facial expressions have an effect on riders.

- Positive reinforcement in the form of a smile is very important in helping students to feel good about themselves and also helps create effective learning environments. Smiling has an important function. For example, if a student about to take an exam walks into a room full of professors with scowls and frowns on their faces the poor student immediately thinks negatively and either turns red or pale. This student has a much lower chance of performing well than another student who walks into a room full of smiling and friendly faces. All creatures can sense negative energy. This negative energy is difficult to diffuse. If people have high positive energy and let this show they can influence others in a wonderful manner.

    Note: Riders can use these same techniques on themselves; a smile will help energy flow in their bodies as well as increasing self-confidence, and can help set a tone for the entire lesson that the instructor can also perceive. A stony-faced rider is more difficult for an instructor to interact with than one who is relaxed and smiling.

APPROPRIATE MOVEMENT IN THE ARENA

- Energy is conveyed from instructor to students. An instructor who moves freely around the ring will initiate a positive energy flow between horse, rider and instructor. Standing still and sitting down for long periods of time can be an energy drain. It is also possible for instructors to move too much; an instructor who constantly trails the student all the way around the arena may cause the horse and/or rider to become nervous and unfocused. At certain times during the lesson having the instructor standing quietly to the side gives the student necessary space to develop "feel" as long as the instructor is not thinking about or focusing on something or someone else (which can be felt by the student and is a distraction). Likewise an instructor with arms folded across the chest closes off the dialogue between horse, rider, and instructor and should be avoided. The instructor can have a powerful influence in the ring through their willingness to use appropriate movement.

GETTING ON THE "SAME PAGE"

- Getting on the "same page" as the horse and rider allows an instructor to see and feel things from their perspective. This includes goals, motives, personality and learning styles, and attitude. Once the instructor is on the rider's page and understands

the rider's individuality, the instructor can use appropriate techniques to help the rider move to a new page if that is necessary for progress. Taking the time to understand the rider's perspective and think about how to help them move forward will be more effective than just commanding the student to do what you want them to do without considering why they are where they are.
- Instructors must also be sure that the student understands the long-term goal and the point of the lesson. When instructors ask questions, they need to listen to the student's answers since this is the best way to find out whether the student has learned the point. If not, the instructor needs to determine where the miscommunication occurred and make every effort to clarify it so that the student goes home with a clear understanding of the point of the lesson.

ENGAGE AND INVOLVE THE STUDENT
- Asking questions of the student and encouraging the student to ask questions is an excellent way to engage and involve the student in the learning process. Creating this atmosphere in a lesson helps the student to be relaxed and better able to 'feel' what the instructor is trying to teach him or her.
- It is also helpful to involve the student in reviews and evaluations. When the student can identify their own strengths and growth areas, they will make faster progress than if they just listen to an instructor's feedback and suggestions. The instructor's ways of communicating with the student will have a large impact on whether a student feels comfortable expressing their opinions during reviews and evaluations.
- Set up situations that help the student get the 'feel' of the topic and then build on this 'feel' using assigned exercises and reminding the student of their own descriptive words for the feeling.

Play and Flexibility

As with any skill, people tend to want to know THE way to teach correctly. The problem is that in riding there is no one way that is correct for all riders, all horses, and all instructors. Riding requires a degree of flexibility and a sense of being willing to play with various methods and exercises in order to achieve particular goals. There may be ten different ways to reach one goal for ten different horse/rider/instructor combinations. This is what makes riding so exciting and interesting. Each learning situation is new and while instructors should be influenced by their experiences in the past, they must be open to trying new things as they help riders advance along the scale of education. The ability to play with information and exercises will probably need to be modeled by the instructor for the student as most students enter the lesson situation wanting to please the instructor and to do things "right." As instructors place more emphasis on awareness than on correctness, students will learn to experiment and think about ways to achieve goals that they think might work best for them. When instructors and students have this kind of open dialogue and flexibility about method, lessons are fulfilling for each of them. Frustration, fear, and aggression are unlikely to appear in these situations, and students will quickly progress into the independent riders with effective seats that instructors wish for!

- Instructors need to be flexible in the lesson topic and learning goals after evaluating the student at the beginning of each lesson. Being prepared with a lesson topic and a plan is essential, but equally essential is the flexibility to modify that plan based on what is happening in the arena at the moment. A rider may arrive for a lesson on a new horse, or having suffered a recent fall, or perhaps the horse is recovering from an injury; all these may require a revision of the lesson topic.
- During the lesson, instructors may discover that a technique is not producing the intended results. When this happens instructors need to try another approach. This may involve a different method of communication or a different exercise to reach the intended result.
- By modeling flexibility during a lesson, instructors will help students learn to be flexible themselves when riding without instruction. Flexibility is a key component of effective riding; riders must be able to try several different approaches to reach their daily goal if the first attempt does not work.

Use of Mistakes

Problems, mistakes, faults; all of these words are commonly used to describe what happens when the horse or rider displays something less than the ideal. However, using negative terms is not effective in helping riders come closer to achieving their individual ideal. Calling something a mistake is only correct when the horse and rider do not make any steps towards achieving the original intention, such as a rider who asks the horse for a canter, but gets no response from the horse. If the rider is in the trot and asks for the canter, but succeeds only in getting a faster trot, this is not a mistake, it is a deficiency. Deficiencies are when some parts of the intention are realized, but some parts still need to be improved or realized. A third term that may be used is "deviation." Deviations are students' attempts to realize their original intention, and may not be correct or be the best way to solve the task given them, but they are not mistakes. Often times the root of those deviations is found elsewhere in the body, so the instructor must be aware of the ways that the rider's body and mind are connected in order to help the rider discover the most effective and efficient solution. For example, a rider who is getting red in the face is not making a mistake, but is probably either holding his breath or becoming frustrated with himself or his horse, two common deviations from the ideal, relaxed, breathing frame of mind and body that is the overall intention or goal. Another example is a rider who is sitting in the chair seat. This is not a mistake, but is a deviation from the ideal, balanced position, perhaps resulting from the rider's attempts to feel secure and in control of the horse.

Instructors are challenged to use deficiencies, deviations, and mistakes as learning experiences, and lead their students to discover ways to make the desired changes.

Use of Exercises

One of the best methods to create awareness in the rider's body or to help a rider really feel a change is through unmounted and mounted exercises. When an exercise results in a change, the rider is more likely to feel what has changed and maybe even to understand what he did to create that change. Awareness through the process of change motivates the rider to continue using that exercise to make the change permanent through practice. Mounted exercises are fairly commonly incorporated into lesson situations, but I have found even more success through using unmounted exercises. Removing the rider from the horse takes away a distraction and also provides the rider with a definite feeling of "before" and "after" when she mounts up again and begins to ride. Quite often the horse is the best reflection of the change in the rider, and it is so much more effective to have a rider smile and say, "I can't believe how much more forward she is going now" after performing an unmounted exercise, rather than having the instructor point out that the horse is now slowly becoming more forward going as the rider positions herself in a certain way while mounted.

Using exercises to create the 'feel' is often worth more than words. Different exercises produce different 'feels' so instructors are encouraged to explore various exercises to discover what works for each individual student and the 'feel' being learned. Several useful exercises are explained throughout the Rider Section. Instructors are encouraged to become familiar with these and also to experiment with their own exercises to help their riders discover the desired feelings for motion.

OFF THE HORSE

Exercises off the horse are excellent as a rider warm-up and to fix problems in specific areas of the body. Once students have experienced the changes to their riding that unmounted exercises can make, they will be more motivated to practice these exercises in between rides. Instructors can encourage students to work on their own body awareness and balance between rides. This saves considerable wear and tear on the horse and speeds up learning while mounted.

ON THE HORSE

During the lesson, instructors may discover a mounted exercise that helps the rider feel a motion or position. Being able to have the student perform the exercise at various times throughout the lesson in order to regain the particular feel is far more valuable to the rider than using verbal commands to talk the rider back to the correct motion or position. Riders will be able to use this exercise on their own in between lessons to practice the desired feel.

Keep it Simple

Students can easily be overwhelmed with commands or tasks if the instructor forgets simplicity in instruction. In order to correctly learn muscle memories students need to learn them one at a time. While maintaining the focus on a particular muscle memory, instructors can incorporate a variety of exercises and tasks for the student to use to develop and practice this skill in order to keep it interesting. Some students want to learn everything all at once, but usually when the instructor explains why it is important to learn one thing at a time, students are content to practice accordingly. Breaking larger, complicated tasks down into smaller, simpler ones will actually result in faster achievement of quality performance in the long run.

When new tasks are introduced, instructors need to give the student permission to make deviations, or even mistakes. Students often want to be told everything that they need to do so that they can do it perfectly from the beginning, but it is actually more to their benefit to hear the basics and then to experiment to discover which aids are necessary to perform the skill. This way the student will associate a feeling with the skill rather than just a set of aids. As the student becomes more comfortable with the new skill instructors can help the student learn to prioritize among the different parts of performing the task, still keeping it simple.

> *Instructors should not overwhelm their students with verbal requirements, but should use multiple methods to convey the necessary information.*

Lessons are Instructional for Instructors Too!
EVALUATING YOURSELF

Carefully planned and carried out lessons should be recognized as such, as well as lessons which did not work out as planned. Every lesson is a learning opportunity for the instructor as well as for the rider. It is important to take the time to evaluate lessons that have been taught; instructors can either train themselves to do this, or can ask an outside observer to give them feedback. The best system for evaluation includes the same criteria that were used for lesson planning. Künneke and Meyners have developed a category system for instructors as motion communicators and as motion teachers, which has been used in many of their conferences and seminars for the "APO" 2000. The APO is a publication put out by the German National Federation which has all of the examination requirements for the various levels of instructors in Germany. The following sections describe this model.

Criteria to Consider When Evaluating a Riding Lesson
- Is the goal of the lesson clear?
- Does the lesson have a good structure that fits with the lesson's goals?
- Is the lesson within the framework of the principles of teaching horseback riding? Have these theories been systematically integrated into the lesson?

- Which principles for physical fitness are considered for rider and horse:
  - Increase in effort intensity?
  - Consideration of effort ability?
  - Consideration of suppleness?
- Appropriateness for the lesson's phases:
  - Greeting
  - Warm-up evaluation (planning phase)
  - Training sets (working phase)
  - Review (cool-down phase)
- Are the strengths and weaknesses of the rider and horse recognized and respected?
- Does the instructor work toward the goal(s) in an appropriate way?
- Does the lesson go as planned or is it more impromptu (intuitive)? Does the content serve the goal?
- Does the instructor give equal and adequate attention to both rider and horse?
- Does the instructor work toward the individual goals set for both rider and horse?
- When does the instructor teach collectively, and when individually (in a group setting)? Is this successful?
- How would the instructor's teaching style be characterized, in general?
- Does the instructor deal with instances of danger or fear? Which measures are then taken to restore order?

Criteria to Consider When Evaluating a Lesson Regarding the Education of the Horse

- Is the Scale of Education (rhythm, looseness, contact, impulsion, straightness, and collection) recognizable in the lesson?
- Are the following gymnastic riding principles implemented?
  - change of gait
  - changing direction for equal skill development on both reins
  - change of tempo
  - work (riding) on bent and curved lines
  - change in the level of the poll and forehand of the horse
  - exercises to develop driving (thrust) and carrying power of the hind legs
- Are the lessons carried out in a systematic way? Are the corrections productive?

- Are difficulties dealt with?
- Is the instructor's location in the riding ring beneficial for corrections?

Criteria to Consider When Evaluating a Lesson Regarding the Education of the Rider

- Is the goal of the lesson clear to the student?
- Are seat and aid corrections holistic (dealing with the entire body) or partial (dealing with only parts of the body)? Are the corrections being made just to the outer form of the rider or to the inner, dynamic motions of the rider?
- Are the instructor's corrections appropriate? Does the student understand them?
- Which methods/exercises/content does the instructor use? Does the instructor clearly implement them according to the rider's skill level?
- Are the instructor's demands in accordance with the rider's experience and skill level?
- Is the instructor's location in the riding ring beneficial for corrections?
- Do the instructor's students regard his or her teaching style highly?
- What kind of words and gestures do the riders use?
- What motivational measures does the instructor incorporate?
- Does the instructor react to and consider suggestions or remarks by his or her students? Does this lead to flexible teamwork?
- Does the instructor discuss the lesson with a student afterwards with effective responses, constructive criticism and/or suggestions for the next lesson?

REFERENCES

Recommended Books in German

ALEXANDER, F.M.:	Der Gebrauch des Selbst. München 1988
BARLOW, W.:	Die Alexander-Technik. München 1993
BRENNAN, R.:	Alexander-Technik. Braunschweig 1995
BRÜGGER, A.:	Gesunde Körperhaltung im Alltag. Zürich 1990, 3. Aufl.
DENNISON, P.E./G.:	Brain-Gym 1 und 2. Freiburg (Breisgau) 1992
DENNISON, P.E./G.:	Das Handbuch der Edu-Kinesthetik für Eltern, Lehrer und Kinder. Freiburg (Breisgau) 1990, 5. Aufl.
DENNISON, P.E./G.:	Lehrerhandbuch Brain Gym. Freiburg (Breisgau) 2001, 11. Aufl.
DENNISON, P.E.:	Befreite Bahnen. Freiburg (Breisgau) 2002, 13. Aufl.
DIAMOND, J.:	Der Körper lügt nicht. Freiburg (Breisgau) 2001, 17. Aufl.
DIAMOND, J.:	Die heilende Kraft der Emotionen. Freiburg (Breisgau) 2001, 12. Aufl.
DRAKE, J.:	Alexander-Technik im Alltag. München 1993
EBERSPÄCHER, H.:	Mentale Trainingsformen in der Praxis. Oberhaching 1990
ENNENBACH, W.:	Bild und Mitbewegung. Köln 1989
FELDENKRAIS, M.:	Bewusstsein durch Bewegung. Der aufrechte Gang. Frankfurt a.M. 1978
FELDENKRAIS, M.:	Die Entdeckung des Selbstverständlichen. Frankfurt 1985
FELDENKRAIS, M.:	Die Feldenkraismethode in Aktion. Paderborn 1990
FELDENKRAIS, M.:	Evolution, Körper und Verhalten. Paderborn 1994

FELLSCHES, J.: (Hg.) Körperbewusstsein. Essen 1991
FLEIß, U.: Unsere Wirbelsäule. Leoben 1988
Frankfurt a.M. 1982
FN (Hg.): Regelwerk für Ausbildung und Prüfung im Deutschen Pferdesport. Warendorf 2000
GALLWEY, W.T.: Tennis. Das innere Spiel. München 1991
GELB, M.: Körperdynamik. Frankfurt a.M./Berlin 1996
GORDIJN, C.C.F.: Sich-Bewegen-ein Dialog zwischen Mensch und Welt
In: Sportpädagogik 3 (1979) 2, 14-19
GRAY, J.: Die Alexander-Technik. Bergisch Gladbach 1992
HANNA, T.: Beweglich sein-ein Leben lang. München 1990
HOMFELDT, H.G. (Hg.): Sinnliche Wahrnehmung, Körperbewusstsein, Gesunderhaltung. Weinheim 1991
HÖLZEL, P. u. W.: Fahren lernen leicht gemacht mit mentalem Training. Warendorf 1997
LEIST, K.-H.: Sich über Wahrnehmungsweisen verständigen. In: Sportpädagogik 14 (1990) 1, 30-37
LEIST, K.-H.: Vom gefühlvollen Sich-Bewegen und seiner Vermittlung. In: Sportpädagogik 14 (1990) 4, 19-25
MEINEL, K./
SCHNABEL, G.: Bewegungslehre-Sportmotorik. Berlin 1998, 9. Aufl.
MEYNERS, E.: Reitpädagogische Grundlagen für den Ausbilder im Reitsport. Hannover 1992
MEYNERS, E.: Erfolgreich reiten. Bewegungsgefühl-das innere Auge des Reiters. Düsseldorf 1996
MEYNERS, E.: Das Bewegungsgefühl des Reiters. Stuttgart 2003
MEYNERS, E.: Lehren und Lernen im Reitsport. Lüneburg 2002, 2. Aufl.
MEYNERS, E.: Exercise Program For Riders. Simple and effective. Huson (USA) 2003
MIESNER, S./MEYNERS, E.: Der Weg zum richtigen Sitz. Warendorf 1997 (Videofilm)
MILZ, H.: Der wiederentdeckte Körper. München/Zürich 1992

NEUMEIER, A.:	Koordinatives Anforderungsprofil und Koordinationstraining. Köln 1999
SCHINKE, B. u. R.:	Erfolgreich reiten mit mentalem Training. Warendorf 1999
SCHNABEL, G./ HARRE, D./ BORDE, A.:	Trainingswissenschaft. Leistung, Training, Wettkampf. Berlin 1997
SWIFT, S.:	Reiten aus der Körpermitte. Rüschlikon-Zürich 1989
TAMBOER, J.:	Menschenbilder hinter Bewegungsbildern. Ins Deutsche übersetzte Habilitation. o. Ort. o. Jahr
TAMBOER, J.:	Sich-Bewegen-ein Dialog zwischen Mensch und Welt. In: Sportpädagogik 3 (1979) 2, S. 14-19
THIE, J.F.:	Gesund durch Berühren. Basel 1990, 7. Aufl.
TOURELLE, M. LA/ COURTNEY, A:	Was ist Angewandte Kinesiologie ? Freiburg i. Breisgau 1998, 5. Aufl.
TREBELS, A.H.:	Bewegen und Wahrnehmen. In: Sportpädagogik 17 (1993) 6, S. 19-27
TREBELS, A.H.:	Bewegung sehen und beurteilen. In: Sportpädagogik 14 (1990/1) 1, S. 12-20
TREBELS, A.H:	Bewegungsgefühl: der Zusammenhang von Spüren und Bewirken. In: Sportpädagogik 14 (1990/2) 4, S. 12-18
TREBELS, A.H.:	Das dialogische Bewegungskonzept. Eine pädagogische Auslegung von Bewegung. In: Sportunterricht 41 (1992) 6, S. 20-29
TREBELS, A.H.:	Bewegen und Wahrnehmen. In: Sportpädagogik 17 (1993) 6, S. 19-227
WEINECK, J.:	Optimales Training. Erlangen 1997, 7. Aufl.

Recommended Books in English

Barlow, W.	*The Alexander Technique*
Dennison, P.E. & G.	Brain Gym information see www.BrainGym.com
Diamond, J.	*Your Body Doesn't Lie,* Warner Books, 1979.
Feldendrais, M.	*Awareness through Movement,* Harper Collins, 1990.
Galloway, W.T.	*The Inner Game of Tennis,* Random House, 1997.
Gray, J.	*The Alexander Technique*, St. Martin's Press, 1991.
Hanna, T.	*The Body of Life,* Healing Arts Press, 1993.
Hanna, T.	*Somatics,* Perseus Books, 1988.
Hannaford, C.	*Smart Moves: Why Learning is Not All in Your Head.* NC: Great Ocean Publishers, 1995.
Meyners, E.	*Exercise Program for Riders.* Goals Unlimited Press, 2003.
Swift, S.	*Centered Riding,* Trafalgar Square, 1985.™

LIST OF EXERCISES

	Figure No.	Page
GENERAL MOTION		
Dynamic Turning on the Long Axis	Fig. 1	50
LEARNING MOTIONS		
Cross-coordination Motions	Fig. 3	60
Sideways Figure Eights	Fig. 4	61
The Elephant	Fig. 5	62
BALANCE		
Tongue to Teeth		70
Changing Stirrup Length		71
"Monkey Posture" (Two-point, Jumping Position)		71
Opposing Motions		73
Jumping Exercises		73
HEAD		
Puppet	Fig. 19	103
Neck Massage and Stretch	Fig. 20-23	103
The Owl	Fig. 24	104
HEAD, NECK, SHOULDERS AND ARMS		
Neck Swing	Fig. 26	107–8
Lengthening the Throat and Neck Muscles	Fig. 27	109
TORSO		
Arm Flow	Fig. 28	111
Strengthening the Oblique Stomach Muscles	Fig. 29-30	112–13
Lengthening the Middle Chest Muscles	Fig. 31	113

Lengthening the Lower Chest Muscles	Fig. 32	114
Strengthening the Muscles— the Side of the Torso	Fig. 33	114
Strengthening the Back Muscles	Fig. 34-35	115
Strengthening the Back Muscles, Buttock Muscles and the Back of the Thighs	Fig. 36	115
Strengthening the Stomach Muscles, especially the Lower Stomach Muscles	Fig. 37	116

PELVIS

Shoulder-Knee Stretch	Fig. 40	118
Crawl to a Sitting Position	Fig. 41	119
Lengthening the Hip Adductors	Fig. 42-44	120
Clock	Fig. 45	121

LEGS

Developing Awareness of the Hamstrings		123
Strengthening the Back of the Thighs and Buttock Muscles	Fig. 47	124
Lengthening the Back of the Thighs and the Calves	Fig. 48	124

RELAXATION

Smiling		137
Humming		137
Deep Breathing	Fig. 65	138
Thumping the Thymus	Fig. 66	138–39
Cobra	Fig. 67	139

Sample Written Lesson Plan (Student Instructor of Eckart Meyners in Germany)

Please note that this is just an *example* of how to prepare a detailed written lesson plan, and even though there are specific learning goals and possible deviations with solutions listed, instructors must always remain flexible when they enter the arena. The process of preparing lesson plans like this is meant to help the instructor be more prepared for whatever they will encounter in the arena, even if it does not exactly match their prepared plan (which it probably will not!).
For this lesson there are no Tools/Media needed.

LESSON TOPIC:
Riding on bending lines to improve the suppleness (position and bend) and to continue development of the carrying power.

LEARNING GOAL:
The rider should
- *change the suppleness of their horse through changes of direction.*
- *work their horse on small bending lines (volte), making position and bend more regular.*
- *in turning, be sure that the diagonal aids are finely in tune with one another.*
- *lead the horse into the turn with the inside rein and then soften it, being sure not to block on the inside rein.*
- *increase the activity of the hindquarters through using an active inside driving leg at the girth.*
- *in turning, make sure their outside shoulder follows appropriately and the rider is sitting in harmony with the entire motion of the horse.*

HORSE / RIDER INFORMATION:
Edna *is forty-one years old; she rode intensively as a junior/young rider, mainly young horses up to Class A. She is a sensitive rider, and this combined with her long break from riding has created challenges for her. It is difficult for her to keep her upper body upright (with positive tension). The middle position must first be strengthened and suppled in order to resonate with the horse. She tends toward a light and uneven rein contact, with the right rein dominating. The driving and restraining aids must be better coordinated.*

Edna's horse *is five years old, possesses a good degree of looseness, is rhythmical and always has a good working attitude. Because of this, it is not so important that her muscles are not yet fully developed. Her conformation is light, and she is not always active enough in her hindquarters, causing her to lean on the rider's hands and be light in the neck.*

Jordan *is twenty-one years old; she is an experienced rider in both dressage and jumping up to Class L, and has trained her own horse to that level. One of her main problems is that she has gotten used to keeping her hands fixed low and closed. She needs to carry her hands more upright in order to be able to more sensitively influence the horse. Occasionally she tends to cause too much tension in her horse because her leg and rein aids are not appropriately coordinated.*

HORSE / RIDER INFORMATION:

Jordan's horse is a ten-year-old who has been successfully competed in dressage and jumping, with an active and spirited motion in the trot and canter. Looseness is not always fully present, therefore the rhythm in the walk is often missing and there is unsteadiness in the contact. In turns, the position and the bend should be further developed, with special attention to keeping the hindquarters from swinging out.

George is thirty-six years old; he is experienced in the education of both younger and older horses. He has a good, upright seat; however, in some situations he lacks suppleness. Therefore he tends to regulate the horse too much with his hand and does not drive enough with the leg. Due to an injury to the lateral muscles in his torso, it is difficult for him to bring his right shoulder with him properly in turns to the left.

George's horse is a fifteen-year-old trained through Class M, and on the way to Class S. She moves with rhythm and swings with a very active and dynamic hindquarter. She is evenly gymnasticized on both hands. Occasionally she shows mental tension and therefore does not have complete looseness, which causes the contact to sometimes be unsteady.

Because the riders and especially the horses show different educational levels, there will be times during the lesson when each is given different tasks in order to address their individual needs.

Nr	Time	Skill/Exercise	Organization	Focus/Learning Goal	Possible Faults/Solutions
1	15 minutes	a) Walking phase of warm-up on long rein.	Riding independently, but all going the same direction.		
		b) Posting trot on large bending lines in working tempo with changes of direction "out of the circle."	Riding one after the other, in a line.	2 beats Even position and bend corresponding to the bending line. Correct outside aids. Stretching forwards/downwards. Improvement of the contact.	Horse's nose not in front of the vertical = Use half-halts always offering the horse a chance to stretch into the contact, and activating the hindquarter through driving.

continued on next page

Nr	Time	Skill/Exercise	Organization	Focus/Learning Goal	Possible Faults/Solutions
		c) In between times, making independent transitions between walk and trot. Transition to the medium walk and check tack (possible tightening of girth).	Riding independently, but all going the same direction.	Even position and bend corresponding to the bending line. Marching, long-strided, purposeful walk. Clear 4 beats. Harmonious "throughness" in transitions.	Transition between trot/walk too abrupt. Transition through pulling on the reins = Use half-halts to better prepare for the transitions, so the rider can give the reins.
		d) Working trot posting. Ride a serpentine of three loops with a change of posting diagonal each time the centerline is crossed.	Riding one after the other, in a line.	See point b). Smooth changes of direction with the inside hand softening. Head and torso turn in the direction of movement.	See under point b). Horse runs over the outside shoulder. Horse is too strongly pulled to the inside = More connection on the outside rein (as a boundary) and always seeking to lighten on the inside rein. Horse falls out with the hindquarters = Use the outside leg as a boundary.
		e) Transition to medium walk.	Riding independently, but all going the same direction.	Marching, long-strided, purposeful walk. Clear 4 beats.	No clear 4 beats. Lowered, tensed fists, too strong hand effect = Go with the movement without giving up support, sensitive driving, with a relaxed middle position. Horse hollows, support gets lost = As above.

SAMPLE — DIAGRAM 5 — Appendix A   197

Nr	Time	Skill/Exercise	Organization	Focus/Learning Goal	Possible Faults/Solutions
2	10 minutes	f) Working trot posting (spread out on two circles); on the open side of the circle, let the horse "chew" the reins out of the rider's hands (stretching circle). Change direction "out of the circle."	Riding independently, but all going the same direction.	Check the looseness. Receive rhythm. Stretching forwards/downwards.	Horse's nose no longer in front of the vertical = Let the reins long again and drive the horse from behind up into the hand. Reins are hanging loose = Take a firmer grip on the reins and keep eyes looking ahead. Rhythm and swing are lost = Use the forward driving aids so that the horse lets itself stretch forwards/downwards into the hand with an even more active hindquarter.
		g) Change between posting and sitting trot.	Riding one after the other. Riding independently, but all going the same direction.	Horse swings in the back. Rider comes to sitting.	Rider does not come to sitting trot = In the posting trot work the horse longer forward/downwards.
		h) Transition to medium walk around the whole arena.		Marching, long stride, purposeful walk. 4 beats.	Look under Set 1. e) for possible faults and corrections for walk.
		i) Working trot spread out on two circles. On the "closed" side of the circle, working canter.		3 beats. Cantering "uphill." Purposeful, long stride. Correct position and bend on the circle line.	Horse leans on the hand, the hindquarters not active. Horse comes onto the forehand = Use more half-halts to activate the hindquarters more and drive the horse upwards to a giving hand so that the horse carries himself more.

Appendix A — SAMPLE — DIAGRAM 5

Nr	Time	Skill/Exercise	Organization	Focus/Learning Goal	Possible Faults/Solutions
3	10 minutes	m) Working trot; make 10-meter circles at pre-determined places in the arena. In between, on the other long side, making independent transitions between trot and walk.	Riding independently but in the same direction.	Correct position and bend corresponding to the volte. Correct outside aids. The inside hind leg steps more underneath the horse.	Horse runs over the outside shoulder = Define the boundary with the outside rein. Horse's hindquarter falls to the outside = Define the boundary with the outside leg aid. Horse is over bent to the inside, which could lead to the above problems as well = Each time the horse accepts the rein aid an allowing must follow so as not to block with the inside rein. Use more diagonal aids.
		n) In between, change directions across the diagonal in posting trot to lengthen the strides.	Riding one after the other, in a line.	Slightly longer frame. Good feeling in the downward transitions.	Horse loses the tempo. Riding forward too suddenly. Rhythm was rushed (horse begins to run) = Gradually increase/decrease the strides without pushing too much with the aids. = Fine tune the use of the aids. = Make the rhythm better through a restraining, slowing upright seat.
		o) Transition to medium walk.	Riding independently but in the same direction.	Marching, long-strided, purposeful, with 4 beats.	See 1 e) for walk.

SAMPLE — DIAGRAM 5 — Appendix A

Nr	Time	Skill/Exercise	Organization	Focus/Learning Goal	Possible Faults/Solutions
		p) Working trot on the long side, from M-B ride in a slight inner position (like a shoulder-fore). George–shoulder-fore, at 'B' ride a 10 m circle, from B-F shoulder-fore. In between on the other long side, ride independent transitions between trot/walk.		2 beats. Correct position and bend.	*Hindquarters falling to the outside* = Guard more with the outside leg. *Horse falls out over the outside shoulder.* *Too much pressure on the inside rein pulls the horse out of position* = More guarding with the outside rein. = Better working together between taking and giving of the inside rein (not continuing to hang on the inside rein). *Hindquarters are allowed to swing through collapsing the hips or over rotating the upper body.* = Rider looks through the horse's ears, and brings the outside shoulder with him/her. = Put weight on the inside seatbone.
		q) In between change directions across the diagonal to lengthen the steps.	Riding one after the other, in a line.	Slightly longer frame. Good feeling in the downward transitions.	See n).

Appendix A — SAMPLE — DIAGRAM 5

Nr	Time	Skill/Exercise	Organization	Focus/Learning Goal	Possible Faults/Solutions
4	10–15 minutes	Rider: Edna Working canter on the circle and make the circle smaller. In between make transitions from canter to trot and from trot to walk. Rider: Jordan Working canter on the circle and make the circle smaller until it is 10-meters, then transition to collected canter and make the circle bigger. Collected canter (around the whole arena). In the middle of the long side ride a volte (8m). In the next corner ride an 8m half-volte and reverse without changing lead.	Individual tasks	Active hindquarter of the horse. Upper body held in proper tone through preparation for transitions. Supple transitions. Even position and bend on the bent line. In the turns and in counter-canter the "jumping through" remains. In the turn soften the inside hand forward. Even position and bend. Shoulder-in on three tracks. Upper body rotates.	Horse leans on the rider's hand. Horse falls onto the forehand = Half-halt. = Stronger driving aids so that the horse canters more uphill. = Rider must maintain the necessary muscle tone in the seat. Horse's hindquarters fall to the outside = Increase the guarding of the outside leg. Horse is not correctly positioned and bent on the bending line = Better coordination of the diagonal aids. = Upper body turns in the direction of movement. = Make sure not to block with the inside rein. Horse is not bent enough in the shoulder-in = Drive more with the inner leg at the girth. Horse is overbent in the lateral movements = Give more with the inside hand. Hindquarter leads in the half-pass = Too strong positioning with the inside rein and too strong driving with the outside leg.

SAMPLE — DIAGRAM 5 — Appendix A   201

Nr	Time	Skill/Exercise	Organization	Focus/Learning Goal	Possible Faults/Solutions
		Rider: George *Collected trot on the right hand, from M-B ride shoulder-in, at B ride volte (8m), then from B-F ride shoulder-in.* *At A turn down the center line and half-pass right to the change points in the arena. Do the same thing on the left rein. In between change rein across the diagonal and ride forward to develop impulsion.*	*Individual tasks*	*Even position and bend.* *Shoulder-in on three tracks.* *Upper body rotates appropriately in the direction of movement.* *In the voltes and half-passes make sure the inside hand gives and does not block.*	*Horse is not bent enough in the shoulder-in* *= Drive more with the inside leg at the girth.* *Horse is overbent in the lateral movements* *= Give more with the inside hand.* *Hindquarter leads in the half-pass = Too strong positioning with the inside rein and too strong driving with the outside leg.* *Horse's hindquarters fall out during the volte* *= More guarding with the outside leg.* *= Bring the upper body more in the direction of motion.* *= Give with the inside rein.*

TOPIC:
Improve "throughness" with an example from skills at 'A' Level

LEARNING GOAL:
The rider should solve the lesson such that the horse becomes "through." The horse should:
- *Obey and freely accept the aids of the rider,*
- *Move in rhythm, balance, and looseness,*
- *Develop more activity in the hindquarters.*

The rider should carefully coordinate the aids (driving and restraining aids).

BACKGROUND ON RIDERS:

Rider: Lisa *is a versatile rider with a focus on jumping. Until now she is not active in competition. Her seat shows several deficiencies. Especially problematic is her collapsing right hip and an unsteadiness in her upper body. These originate from a tightness in her pelvis. Lisa's strength lies in her learning and achievement abilities and in her inner calmness and composure when working with her horse.*

Horse: Wonderwoman, *12-year-old grey mare. Her early training was versatile and then she had a break for foaling. Since 1999 she has been regularly under saddle again and is solid up to level A. Her problem is straightness and the general tendency to lose rhythm; this is also reinforced through Lisa's seat problems (hips). Therefore, this must remain the focus point in her work with regard to throughness.*

Rider: Andy *rides in all three disciplines (dressage, show jumping and eventing) to level M. However, his priority is all-around riding. He has a lot of experience with many different types of horses. However, he is sometimes a little impatient.*

Horse: Alycia, *4-year-old brown mare, versatile, talented, trained to level A. She shows basic level L training as well. Her natural trot and canter are above average and she has a good work ethic. Her walk is not always balanced and therefore sometimes she loses rhythm.*

Nr.	Exercise	Focus Point	Possible Deviations
1	Posting trot on the circle, trot/walk transitions, trot/canter transitions in both directions	- Looseness through the gaits and the changes of tempo - Beginning to work on bending	- Too strong rein aids (especially the inside rein) - Lack of steadiness - Unclear circle line
2	Trot around whole arena, serpentine through the entire arena, at the crossing of the center line transition to walk and after that on a straight line with lighter reinforcement	- Throughness, beginning bending, beginning understanding of changes between pushing and carrying power	- Loss of forward movement - Wrong route

SAMPLE — DIAGRAM 6 — Appendix B

Nr.	Exercise	Focus Point	Possible Deviations
3	From the center line move away from the leg (right and left), and then a short trot phase to finish	- Support throughness, coordination of supporting aids	- Loss of forward movement - Wrong route
4	Walk-Canter transitions on the circle in both directions	- Correct position and bend - Activate hindquarters	- Canter through trot - Running through half-halts - No clear walk steps - Falling out over the shoulder
5	Simple change of canter lead out of the circle	- Smooth transition, clear walk steps, good preparation for the new canter	- Not changing to the new lead - Too few or too many walk steps

TOOLS/ACCESSORIES
- Mark the circle lines with cones
- Mark the serpentine with cones
- Use poles to show/describe the optimal straight line of the horse when riding across the centerline

ORGANIZATION: *Individual riding*

TRAINING AND EXERCISE SUGGESTIONS FOR INDEPENDENT WORK:
- Medium range continuation of this work until widening of the following lessons
- Emphasize the forward driving aids (with awareness of the restraining aids)
- Reinforce on bending lines

THOUGHTS FOR THE NEXT LESSON:
- Application of the gymnasticizing principles to changing the way of going, often changing directions, varying the tempo, changing the horse's position

INDEX

Active Learning, 149; definition of, 6,11; how riders learn, 18-19
Aggression, 86-93; effect of instructor on, 152, 181
Agility: coordination and, 7, 8, 16, 41, 44-45; development stages, 152-156
Aids: aggression and, 87; clock exercise, 121; content analysis of lesson and, 158; cyclical and non-cyclical motions, 47; dialogue, 31, 36, 38; driving, 110; fear and, 85; holisitic approach, 34; hollow back, 118; individuality, 17, 144; influences on, 44; legs, 122; pelvis, 116; planning and, 21; posture, 130; power and, 52; "questions" and, 35; range of motion, 53; seat, 97, 98, 100; "trigger aids", 166; verbal description of, 167
Alignment: balanced and elastic, 96; posture, 137; seat, 94
Anxiety, 81, 83, 84, 90; aggression and, 90; coordination and, 44; fear and, 79, 81, 83, 84; grimacing, 78
Attitude: frustration, 89; of instructor towards learning, 176; of instructor towards student, 179; positive, 78
Awareness, 26; emphasis on by instructor, 181; fear, 85; inner and outer, 76; of hamstrings, 123; psychology of mind, 75; spatial perception, 43; use of exercises to increase, 183

Balance, alignment and, 96; between horse and rider, 33, 35, 51; cogwheel, 133; coordination and, 42-43; development of in infancy, 153; development of in early childhood, 154; development of in late childhood, 155; driving aids, 123; exercises off the horse to improve, 183; feel and, 161; head and, 102, 105; individuality, 16; kinesiology, 57; motion and, 56; pelvis and, 116; power and, 52; rider, 38; riding as a game of, 64-74; rhythm, 53; saddle and, 136; warm up, 141
Balimo chair, 121
Behavior: aggressive, 86-93, 152; changes in late adulthood, 158; direct learning, 161; fear, 85; "ideal", 145; independent learning, 39; learning goals, 148; one-dimensional viewpoint of, 32; reaction and 149-150
Brain, 4, 6; conscious actions and, 19; deep breathing and, 138; development in infancy of, 153; feeling and, 24, 165, 167, 170; kinesiology, 58; left brain, 21-23, 42, 61, 79, 125;middle age, 157; motion and, 25, 26; opposing motions and, 73; right brain, 21-23, 46, 61; visualization, 164; water, need for, 29

Childhood, early, 154; influences of, 17, 41, 63, 83, 128 late, 154-155; middle, 154; pre and early teens, 155

Cogwheel, 96, 133
Commands: aggression, 87, command-oriented, 5, 10, 11-12, 18, 20, 33, 35, 40, 75, 80, 83, 85, 89, 105; dialogue, 160, 31; instructor and, 149, 161, 180; unnecessary, 168; use of metaphors instead of, 170; visual aids and, 169
Communication, aids and, 163; as dialogue, 31, 67, 35-36; between horse and rider, 35, 107, 110; between horse, rider and instructor, 5, 13, 37, 180, 160, 166; feel and, 24; negative communication, 78; relaxation and, 76; skills, 177-187; tension and, 79; warm-up and, 140
Concentration, balance and, 64; breathing and, 138; environmental influence on, 30; focus and, 76, 101; observation and mental training and, 164
Content, didactic reasoning in lessons and, 160; of lessons, 147-148, 152, 158, 159, 160, 173
Coordination, agility and, 8, 41-44; cross-coordination, 51, 60, 61, 62, 126, 132; definition of, 16; developmental states and, 152-158; fitness and, 6-7; individuality and, 15; use of incorrect aids, 35

Decision making: active learning, 18; fear and, 80; instructor as decision maker, 147; self-initiated riding and 38
Developmental phases, 152-159
Deviations, feel and, 21, 22; in rider, 16; kinesiology, 57 muscle imbalances and, 67; of head, neck, shoulder and arm, 104; of head position and use, 101; of legs, 122; of pelvis, 116; of seat, 100, 101; of torso, 110; mistakes and, 18, 19, 95, 168, 169, 172, 173, 182, 184; sources of, 59, 95, 134
Dialogue: between rider and horse, 16, 36, 37, 38, 67, 102, 149, 160, 161, 165; between rider, horse and instructor, 37, 38, 93, 179, 181; feeling and, 24, 126; holistic approach and, 40; inner dialogue, 166, 167; pelvis and, 116; riding as dialogue, 31-32; saddle fit and, 135; seat and, 94, 96, 110, 135
Disruptions to learning, 10, 35

Education, continuing, 177; individuality and, 15; Scale of Education, 145, 181, 186
Energy: environment, effect on, 30; from instructor to student, 179; kinesiology and, 56; negative, 78, 178, 179; nutrition and, 28; smiling and, 178, 179; tongue to teeth, 70, 71
Environment, holistic method and, 160; influences of, 29, 30, 43, 63, 76, 81, 82, 128, 134, 139, 152; learning environment, 28, 39, 57, 137, 166, 177, 179; unproductive learning environment, 228
Evaluation: didactic reasoning, 159; instructor self-evaluation, 185-187; of learning goals, 149-150; student self-evaluation, 180
Experience-oriented method of instruction, 11, 12-13, 90

Fear, 11, 78, 79-85, 123; failure leading to, 83; general anxiety, 81; of anticipation, 82; of failure, 83, 84; of things, 82; of unknown, 82; orientation problems, 81; sources of, 82

"Feel": aggression and, 88, 89, 91, 93; characteristics of motion and, 52; coordination and agility and, 7, 8; clock exercise to develop, 121-122; deviations and mistakes, 21, 22, 134; dialogue between horse and rider, 37; direct learning and, 161; engaging and involving student, 180; environmental influences on, 29, 30; exercises to develop "feel", 182-183; experience-oriented learning and, 12, 13; "feeling" words, 177; gestures and emotions, 178; holistic approach, 33, 166; hollow back and, 118; improving development of feel, 168-171; individuality and, 15; "inner eye" and, 3; inner/outer matching, 59; instructor and "inner riding", 3; instructor as mediator of motion, 3; internal focus, 171; intuitive riding, 23, 24; letting go, 79; muscle memory, 4, 5, 163; observation and, 27, 165-166; opposing motions, 73-74; posture and, 126, 127, 129, 130; smiling, 137, 179; teaching students to feel, 167; tone of voice, 178

Fitness, 6-7, 15, 16, 33, 60, 112; adulthood, 157; late childhood, 155

Flexibility, 7, 15, 44, 45, 76, 95, 100, 101, 136; developmental stages and, 152-158; lesson planning and, 146, 181; play, 180

Focus, 10, 32, 34, 41, 59, 62, 76, 78, 101, 104; focusing student internally, 171; learning goals and, 172-173; lesson structure and, 174

Goals, 3, 15, 17, 22, 24, 27, 28, 34, 37, 39, 40, 44, 47, 68, 69, 76, 87, 90, 92, 93, 95, 141; didactic reasoning and, 159; evaluation of lesson, 185-186; holistic instruction, 160; lesson planning, 143, 147-148, 149, 151-152, 163, 172-173, 175-176, 181; long term, 146, 175, 180; methods for achieving, 162; observation and, 166; orientation, 18, 20, 21; teens and, 156

Hands, 43, 50, 52, 59, 60, 62, 104, 138
Harmony, with horse, 149, 165
Holistic perspective, 23, 32, 33, 34, 40, 56; dialogue concept, 160-163; function 106; methods of instruction, 188
Humming, 61, 137-138

Independent, 5, 12, 21, 34, 37, 39; learning goals and, 149; teaching with respect, 165, 181; training and exercise suggestions, 173
Infancy, 152
Inner eye, 3, 59, 101
Integration, 74, 84; lesson plans, 145, 185

Kinesiology, 56-58, 137

Learning, active, 18, 19; aggression and, 90-93; decision making, 147; developmental stages and, 152-159; environmental influences, 29-30, 137, 178-179; fear and, 79-84; independent learning, 39; kinesiology and, 58-59; learning, direct, 160-161; motion and, 24-26, 37, 41-42, 57; motivation and, 27-28; nutrition, 28 29; observation and, 26-27; opportunities, 36; process, 19-22,

37, 38; self-awareness and, 75; teaching styles, 177, 180, 181; use of imagery, 170

learning goals, 148-150, 152, 162, 163, 172-173, 175, 181

learning styles, 145, 179

learning to feel, 127, 134, 155, 165

Leg, 9; balance and, 66; choice of aids and, 20; correct position of, 122; developmental stages and, 152-159; hamstrings and, 123; influences on coordination of horse's, 44; monkey posture, 72; range of motion, 53; rider proportions and, 134-135; saddle fit and, 136; seat and, 94, 97, 98; strength of motion, 53; "switching", 126

Lengthening: of chest muscles, 113-114; of hamstrings, 45, 124; of hip adductors, 120; stretching and, 68-69, 98, 109, 154

Lesson, 3, 5, 7, 9, 12, 13; command-oriented, 35, 38, 40; content analysis of, 158-159; creativity and inventiveness, 163; demographics and, 151-152; development stages and, 152-159; dialogue concept, 160-161; didactical reasoning, 159; direct learning, 161-162; exercising before and between, 69; flexibility and, 180-181; goals, 144; holistic approach, 160-161, 162; kinesiology, 57; long term planning, 146, 180; motion in learning, 25, 26; motivation of rider, 28-30; organizational methods, 159; planning, 144, 145, 147-150, 172-175; rider individuality and, 16, 17, 21; requirements of, 151; self-evaluation, 185-187; to develop "feel", 168-171

Methods, 5, 9, 11-13; achieving goals, 162; active learning, 149; communication, 35; child rearing, 83; creativity and inventiveness, 163; development of "feel", 168-171; dialogue concept and, 160; direct learning, 161; experience-oriented, 90; holistic, 160; one-dimensional, 34; organizational methods, 159; S-H-R-S, 68; teaching, 33, 40, 57, 82, 89, 144-145

Mind: and body connection, 33, 34, 75, 78, 94, 95, 96; complexity of, 22; external influences on, 44; fear and, 82; kinesiology and, 57; relaxation and, 136, 139

Mistakes: definition of, 95; fear and, 85; learning and, 18-22, 24, 38; letting go of, 78; recognizing, 55, 167; use of, 181-182, 184

Monkey posture, 72-73

Motivation, 15, 18, 21, 27-28, 165-166; long-term goals and, 174

Motion: agility and, 41, 44-45; analysis of, 55; anticipation of, 45-46; athletic structure of, 46-47; balance and, 56, 65-67; body structure and, 98-100; brain and, 22-24, 79; cadence of, 53; characteristics of, 52-55; clock exercise, 121-122, 133; combining, 49-52; communication and, 35-36, 167; consistency, 54; coordination and, 16, 41-44; cross-coordinated, 126; cyclical, 47-48; developmental phases and, 152-158; dynamic, 134; feeling the, 22, 161, 171; head and, 102, 105, 107; homolateral, 125; holistic perspective of, 34, 40, 163, 166; iliosacral joint and, 116-117; jumping, 74; kinesiology, 56-58; learning and, 24-26, 37-39,

41-63; leg position and, 122, 123; non-cyclical, 48; observation and, 27, 31, 164-166; one-dimensional perspective of, 32-33; opposing, 73, 169-170; pelvis and, 106, 107, 116; posture and, 126-132; precision of, 55; range of, 53; rhythm and, 53; saddle fit and, 136; seat and, 97, 160; stirrup length and, 71

Muscle, 33, 34; agility and 44-45; basic motor skills and, 42; combining motions and, 49; coordination, 42; development phases and, 152-158; effects of smiling, 76; fear and, 85; feeling and, 22, 23; imbalances in, 67; individuality and, 15-16; kinesiology, 57; legs, 123-124; neck 101-102, 105-106; pelvis, 117; physical balance and, 64-67; seat, 94, 96; S-H-R-S method, 68; strengthening, 69-70, 112; stretching, 67-69; water and, 29; weak 35

muscle memory, 4, 5, 25-26, 27, 37-38, 163, 175, 184

Neck: occipital joint and, 77; head and, 101-106; posture and, 129-131; relaxing, 61-62; seat and, 94, 100, 101; shoulder and, 106-108; tension, 59

Nutrition, 28-29

Occipital joint, 77, 102-103, 131
Observation, external, 33; of self (inner), 22, 40; role of, 26-27, 54; visualization, 164-167

Pelvis: clock exercise, 121-122; cogwheel, 133; effect of stirrup length on, 100; individual structure of, 16, 98, 135; position of, 116-118; relaxation of, 66; saddle fit and, 135-136; seat and, 94, 96, 97; tension, 59, 78, 106, 107

Planning: content analysis of lesson and, 158; didactical reasoning and lesson, 159; lesson, 144, 146, 147-150; written lesson plans, 172-175

Position, 3, 5, 6, 8, 12; head and, 51, 101, 106; individuality and, 16-17, 98; Monkey posture, 72-73; muscle balance and, 67; of legs, 122; of pelvis, 116; of shoulders, 104; of torso, 110; stirrup length and, 71

Posture, 125; alignment and, 97; chest and, 104; cross-coordination and, 51; head and, 51, 102, 106, 137; late childhood, 155; Monkey posture, 71-73; muscle balance, 67; neck and, 106; seat and, 100, 134; stress, 126; tension and, 107; torso and, 110, 117; unmounted, 125, 133

Principles of learning, 5

Psychology, 58, 141; awareness, 75; effects of criticism, 90; individuality and, 33; influence on riding, 75-78; kinesiology, 57-58; of learning, 79; what instructors need to know, 176

Questions, 5, 13; dialogue between horse and rider, 32, 35; engaging student with, 180; instructor feedback, 162; lesson review, 175

Relaxation: aggression, 91; back muscles and, 127; balance and, 66; engaging student and, 180; exercises to promote relaxation, 136-140; fun, 76; incorrect posture and, 129, 131, 132; legs,

123; occipital joint and, 77, 102; saddle fit, 136; seat and, 96, 107; S-H-R-S, 68; stretching, 68

Rhythm: balance and, 43, 67; breathing and, 130, 138; cadence of motion, 53, 54; coordination and, 42; early childhood, 154; late childhood, 155; leg, use of, 123; of horse, 102, 107, 127, 133, 135, 136, 160, 162; relaxation and, 76; riding and, 24

Shoulder: agility and, 45; fear and, 77; Monkey posture, 72-73; posture and, 125, 129-130; seat, 96, 100, 110, 111; twisting and, 51

Simple, 84, 184

Smile: positive learning environment, 137, 178, 179; positive reinforcement, 179; relaxation and, 76, 101

Speed, 6, 9; cadence of motion, 52-53

Strength, 3, 7; correct practices, 68-70, 112; hamstrings, 123; hollow back and, 118; individuality and, 16, 59; isometrics, 69; kinesthetic judgment, 43; of motion (power), 52; relaxation and, 104; seat and, 111; stretching, 68-69

Stress, 10; fear, 85; humming, 131-138; positive thinking, 77-78; posture and, 125-126; thumping the thymus, 139; tongue to teeth, 71; water and, 29

Suppleness and agility, 44-45; stirrup length and, 100

Task, 3, 12; active learning 18, 19 21; behavior/action 149; deviations and, 182; focusing student through use of, 171; holistic approach to, 160; simple, 184

Teaching styles, 10, 177-184

Technical, 13; qualifications to teach, 176

Theory, 6, 11, 14, 16; active learning, 18; aggression/learned behavior, 90, 92; "correct" seat, 16; discussion of, in lesson, 175; "feel" and, 22; frustration/aggression, 86; kinesiology, 57

Tightness, 6; psychological stress and, 135; smiling, 101

Topic: flexibility in lesson, 181; goals and contents of lessons, 147-149, 151; lesson planning and, 172; teaching tools for, 150

Torso: breathing and, 138; correct position of, 110; posture and, 131; using correctly, 49-50

Visual aids, 165, 169
Visualization, 3,4; self-observation, 27, 164-165
Voice, tone of, 178

Warm-up, 7, 140-141

BALIMO®
Balance in Motion

This unique chair allows unrestricted natural but complex 3 dimensional motion while having to maintain balance. This freedom of movement in balance is possible due to a specially designed tilt and turning point (patent pending). With this chair you can identify and correct problems in your pelvis area that will translate directly to becoming a better rider.

BENEFITS ARE:
- to mobilize and extend mobility in the hips and pelvis
- to activate and revitalize vertebras through gentle but complex motion
- to train and reconnect muscles along the spine, head and neck area
- to integrate and train the autonomic muscle and nervous system
- to reconnect neural pathways
- to sharpen your senses and increase your confidence
- to support the digestive system

YOU CAN USE BALIMO:
- at home
- in the office
- during training
- whenever there is time to sit down

For more information contact Equestrian Education Systems, Inc.: equestrianedu2@aol.com or 406-626-1947.

ABOUT THE AUTHOR

Author Eckart Meyners demonstrates one of his techniques to student Anne Hornbeak. —PHOTO COURTESY OF RICHARD LUSTHUIS

Eckart Meyners, a professor of sports physiology and movement at the Institute for Leisure Research, Play and Movement Education at the University of Lüneburg, Germany, conducts research on improving athletic performance. Meyners has worked with the German National Equestrian Federation for 25 years, and has been instrumental in developing the progress of equestrian instruction/methodology, and rider training in Germany. Over the years he has developed a series of simple, easy movements to address "blockage" in the rider's body that may interfere with the horse's motion or impede proper communication between horse and rider. Meyners' techniques are easy to learn and easy to do and, best of all, they work.